MIND KIND

Dr Joanna North is a Doctor of Psychotherapy, a Chartered Psychologist and a Chartered Scientist with 30 years of experience working with children, adults and families. She lives in the UK where she works as an expert witness for the Family Court and runs a private clinical practice. Her previously published books are *How to Think About Caring for a Child with Difficult Behaviour* (2010) and *Mindful Therapeutic Care for Children* (2014). Jo has been recognized by the British Psychological Society with the 2017 CPS Distinguished Contribution to Psychology in Practice Award for her work with adopted children.

MIND KIND

Your child's mental health

Dr Joanna North

EXISLE
PUBLISHING

First published 2019

Exisle Publishing Pty Ltd
PO Box 864, Chatswood, NSW 2057, Australia
226 High Street, Dunedin, 9016, New Zealand
www.exislepublishing.com

A CiP record for this book is available from the National Library of Australia.

ISBN 978 1 925335 94 1

Designed by Enni Tuomisalo
Illustrations by Tamsin Carter
Typeset in PT Serif, 10pt
Printed in China

This book uses paper sourced under ISO 14001 guidelines from well-managed forests and other controlled sources.

10 9 8 7 6 5 4 3 2 1

Note

This book is derived from an edition of *Mind Kind* published by Dr Joanna North in 2016. The material has been fully revised and updated for this edition.

Disclaimer

This book is a general guide only and should never be a substitute for the skill, knowledge and experience of a qualified medical professional dealing with the facts, circumstances and symptoms of a particular case. The nutritional, medical and health information presented in this book is based on the research, training and professional experience of the author, and is true and complete to the best of their knowledge. However, this book is intended only as an informative guide; it is not intended to replace or countermand the advice given by the reader's personal physician. Because each person and situation is unique, the author and the publisher urge the reader to check with a qualified healthcare professional before using any procedure where there is a question as to its appropriateness. The author, publisher and their distributors are not responsible for any adverse effects or consequences resulting from the use of the information in this book. It is the responsibility of the reader to consult a physician or other qualified healthcare professional regarding their personal care. This book contains references to products that may not be available everywhere. The intent of the information provided is to be helpful; however, there is no guarantee of results associated with the information provided.

This book is dedicated to anyone who wants to pay attention to the task of parenting and help their children grow healthy minds.

Contents

Introduction

In my work as both a researching psychologist and practicing psychotherapist, engaging with clients both privately and within health services, I am faced with parents who are confounded and upset by their child's state of mind. It seems that because a mental health condition is not a visible form of illness we often don't know how to manage it, and parents can easily become anxious. This kind of upset and confusion from a parent does nothing to help a child who is struggling with mental health issues. It often makes them more worried. These issues do not occur in any particular type of family. Anxiety, stress and resulting mental health conditions appear in all family groups: rich, poor, middle class, working class, stepfamilies, high-functioning families, single-parent families, adopted families, lesbian and gay-parent families. Nor do these conditions relate to any particular gender, race, culture or religion. Our behaviours, values and ways of thinking affect our mental health.

I wrote this book to address the complex task of being a parent today, with the aim of helping you to sustain wellbeing and positive mental health for your child or children. It is also written with the goal of raising awareness of common psychological health issues and how to manage them in children. This book is not a replacement for mental health services. If you are concerned about your child's mental health, you need to take advice from clinical experts including your doctor and mental health services. You may, however, still be worried about your child's mental health and you might want to learn more about what to do and how to think to support your child. If so, this book is written for you. But it is also for any parents who want to engage in skilful care that will inoculate their children against stress, depression and anxiety, obsessive compulsive tendencies, social phobia and separation anxiety, all of which are the most common mental health conditions found in children today.

There are some common parenting misunderstandings about mental health that this book will hopefully help you to clarify. For example, we will look at the tendency to push children towards achievement as a measure of their self-esteem when there are many other measures and reassurances on which we can draw. Parents also have to ask themselves whose self-esteem they are trying to raise — their own or that of their children? However, tiger mums and dads need not put the book down here, because despite this we do need to achieve and it is helpful for our kids to have good exam results. But we do not have to ignore or destroy our wellbeing or theirs in the process. We live in an achievement-based culture and we cannot withdraw from that, but we can inoculate young people against the despair that they may feel when faced with a barrage of achievement-based expectations on which they believe their futures depend. What we really need to be able to do is help our children face this contradiction both within themselves and within society. Do you feel equipped to help your child face this complexity? Indeed, do you feel you are able to face this yourself? One of the hard-hitting facts of this book is that what you are unable to face in yourself, you are unlikely to be able to help your children resolve for themselves. Here is lesson one — it is the most fundamental lesson of parenting and it is one with which parents often need support to accept. Until you are resolved on your issues, your child cannot be either.

What is also challenging for families, and particularly for parents, is when they are doing their very best but still their child is suffering with mental pain or behavioural difficulty and they do not know what to do next to put this right. They immediately want to know what action they can take or what action somebody else can take in remedy. What they really need is to understand why this is happening. The book will nurture this understanding so that you can more calmly move forward towards healthy behavioural goals that enhance life, as well as move away from the behaviours that make a child feel they are carrying a terrible burden or grappling with the legacy of confusion over behaviour in our current world. Much anxiety and depression has its origin in responses to social pressure and expectation that is unreasonable and impossible. Children become separated from reality in a quest to achieve impossible standards of perfection, developing a kind of false self very much divorced from any real and solid sense of who they are. Creating secure children with strong identities will be a continuous theme throughout this book.

We are programmed to raise children in the best possible way for their survival, through responding to their needs and keeping them safe, but there remain many questions about how to do this and parents always want to know the 'best' way. All over the globe, constructive parenting behaviours are replicated time and time again. Children are loved, fed, clothed, educated and supported to grow into autonomous and independent individuals who feel they have a place within society. Despite this, children will also survive and succeed against the most enormous odds such as poverty, domestic violence, neglect, abuse, natural disaster and war-torn environments. Nobody is paid for completing this task, which is an instinctive act of our evolutionary inheritance but at the same time an enormous call on an adult's heart, time and resources. Along the journey as their child develops, parents and carers will be faced with challenges that cause them anxiety and they wonder about the best way to go forward. In western society you will even be sold products to help you raise happy, healthy children. You can buy a potty that sings to your child as they train to use the toilet — probably the most momentous act of self-control and self-management that any toddler has to face. You can buy toys that will educate children as they play, computers to teach vocabulary to under-fives, and it is likely that your toddler has more confidence with your iPad than you do. There are also super-foods that give your children something extra to help them along and there are infinite choices to be made about the best feeding plan for your child. They must not be too fat and they must have enough exercise. They must also not be too thin or develop an eating disorder that distorts their relationship with food for the rest of their life. How on earth do parents ever feel that they are getting any aspect of their child's care right or that they have the control and skill to help them on their path?

In addition to this, there are an infinite number of professionals who will tell you decisively about how you should behave as a parent and what style of parenting you should adopt to achieve the best possible outcome. Polarized advice will be meted out, from swaddling or wrapping your baby to make them feel secure, to not wrapping your baby in anything tight because it is bad for their physical development. I remember wrapping my fractious baby in a shawl just like it said in the book, thinking that I had overcome this frustrating episode with her, only to find she had worked her way out of the wrapping within minutes and freed her own little fist. The poor little thing moved from being fractious to really angry with me! That moment taught me that my baby's fussing was her way of communicating to me that I needed to accept and resolve rather than bring to a halt. Once I could live with her unsettled episodes I came to know her better as a little being struggling to cope with her new experiences — naturally she was fretful at times, and at these times she needed me to accept those communications with as much kindness and tolerance as possible.

It was then that I started to learn that the key was not what I did so much as what I thought and conveyed to her. I had a growing sense that the answer to her wellbeing was in the culture that I created in which she could grow with a sense of loving acceptance. I should point out here that if you think I am writing this book because I got parenting right all the time, you would be wrong. I absolutely did not, and I write this book with the strong desire to have made a better job of this task.

I can only tell you that I parented under very difficult circumstances as a single parent with no support from family but, fortunately, the kindness of a few close friends. My daughter is now 32 and is a beautiful young woman who is well balanced and secure, and who easily brings positive emotions into her life and relates in a very coherent way to others. She is doing the job that she has chosen to do, working as a child counsellor, and she has her own children. I think she has a strong desire to help children to be better understood during the process of childhood, and there is no doubt in my mind this stems from the sense that she was supported with as much skill as I could muster, but at times she may not have felt understood. I did not fully understand my child as she grew up and this can sometimes be a source of regret. There were things about her life I wish I could have dealt with better. However, we now share a joint goal. She works beautifully and creatively with children, helping them to feel confident and giving them a sense of their right to have their voices heard, while I work to educate parents so that they know how to help and think about their children, do not live with regret about their parenting, can feel proud of the efforts they have made, and can enjoy more beautiful moments with their child.

This is not an academic book, although it could be. I have given myself free licence to draw on both established science and research to inform my writing as well as my experience as a practitioner and a parent. I also have a wonderful husband who has been a stepfather to my daughter and a father to two sons. I know that he, too, has had to grow as a parent and even though our children are now fully grown we are still developing and learning about both the past and the present with our children.

A philosophy of parenting

As a professional and as a mother, I know that much advice will be given to you at every moment of your parenting journey. The contradictions are endless and some advice is just plain wrong, given out by individuals who have no evidence for their assumptions or by people simply following the latest craze; sometimes advice is given by people without any experience at all of the demands of caring for children. If you occasionally get confused by conflicting evidence and worry about which way to go, then this book may be a relief to you. This book is not about technique, but rather a set of coherent values — a philosophy of parenting.

In this endeavour I attempt to address the common issues of parenting in our fast-paced, information-based, industrial, financially insecure, materialistic, demanding and very sophisticated society. It is also likely to meet with aspects of parenting outside of the western industrial model of thought and action — parenting in the developing world and parenting through war, want, natural disaster and displacement. I say this because ultimately the rules of parenting are made for us all under all circumstances. There is no one set of parents somewhere getting the whole thing exclusively right, but I think we all carry that myth with us. The value systems I propose draw on evolutionary psychology, theories of counselling and psychotherapy, developmental psychology, philosophy and sociology. Such values also build on the pool of knowledge and experience I have gained in being asked to help parents who have made serious mistakes in their parenting, in my job as a psychotherapist and psychologist and Assessor for the Family Court in Britain, as well as looking at parents who can be considered to be doing a very acceptable job at raising their children.

There is, of course, plenty of ground in between, from insufficient and abusive parenting to tolerable and acceptable levels of supportive care that helps children reach their developmental goals. This middle ground still consists of mistakes, errors and misconceptions on the part of many parents and carers — this is a normal part of learning to raise a child. In my view, this is the ground full of information about what you should do at any given moment. Yet parents still feel insecure and, not surprisingly, frightened when children appear to collapse into states of mind that they struggle to make sense of. Very few parents intend to, or wish to, make errors in their parenting and when they do it is usually due to stress, lack of information or lack of support rather than any deliberate intention. I cannot forget that there is a small percentage of parents who harm through deliberate intention and in our media-based society we hear about these issues too frequently. These stories of cruelty unsettle normal, healthy parents, leaving them anxious and concerned about what can go wrong in the parenting of their child.

My approach

This book intends to give you clear guidance about making good choices in bringing up your child. If your child is struggling with mental health issues I don't think there is a cure-all strategy that will put everything right in your family life. Most therapeutic endeavour to put things right results in good planning and a willingness to be flexible in thinking, so that you can adopt new behaviours and feel more confident about supporting your child in just the right way for them through any period of adversity. The absolute answers that people seem to seek when they approach mental health services do not exist. You are unlikely to get a concrete solution because human beings and their minds are so much more complicated than concrete. What you really need to do at these times is be more aware of your child's mind and what is happening for them so that you can provide emotional support rather than thrashing around, desperately clinging to snippets of misinformation and getting upset and panicky, falling into a cycle of dysregulation with your child. Throughout the book I aim to help you do this.

I may appear hard hitting in places — I think there is much information about parenting that is not discussed fully or frankly because it is uncomfortable. We should be clear about what is just plain wrong and not good enough for children. To help you with this I feel you should be supplied with a sense of where to look if things are difficult for your child. Let's start to face this now. Rather than attacking your child's behaviour, one of the places to look for clues is in your own life and what might be going on within your family context that is affecting your child. Many people are affronted by this and yet within mental health services it is the main clue to a vast number of the cases we see. Is nobody telling you this? The truth is that the environment you build, emotionally and mentally, within your home and in your relationship with your child affects their mental health. Are you able to accept this proposition? If you are, then this book will be very useful to you in helping you build your skills and resources for a healthy emotional environment. If you are not able to accept this idea, this book may also be useful to you as it may help you understand why it is so fundamental to mental health.

For example, what do parents do when they are going through a period of adversity in their relationship and the fallout from that affects their children, causing anxiety? How much does parental break-up affect children and how do we resource them to cope? How much time do you really need to give to your kids to keep them happy? These conundrums exist in the hearts of many parents, keeping them quietly worried so that they miss opportunities for sharing joy and contentment with their children. The place to look for the origins of wellbeing and security is in your own mind, from where you communicate to your child your sense of the world. If you are afraid, they are afraid. They are exact mirrors of the environment you create around them. In this book let's start to look here, rather than trying to find some rare disorder that may magically explain a child's despair or behaviour.

Having said that, of course there are exceptions, because life is full of complexity and chaos, so there are some conditions in children that are not directly related to their parental relationship. To be clear, some mental health conditions are rooted in and fed by the neurological structure of the brain, such as autism or ADHD. In these conditions, parents face challenges that will affect their child's behaviour and responses. This is where parents have to be extra smart about the environment they create for their child, who is vulnerable. Children born with autistic spectrum disorders are a unique challenge to parents and require a lot of sure-footed parenting behaviours. Autistic children are as beautiful as any other child. They just have a different way of seeing the world. They deserve exactly the same chances as any other and require the same, if not more, commitment from their parents. Like any other child, a lack of commitment to that parenting will mean a child collapses into a meaningless world of turmoil, with limited opportunities for reaching constructive goals and often disastrous consequences around behaviour and social inclusion. Perhaps here is our first clue to the type of parenting I am trying to promote. Our first word: commitment. You can't do a half-job. You have to be there, whatever the neurological make-up of your child, whatever is going on.

The Mind Kind approach to parenting

Along with commitment, I advocate a more mindful approach to parenting. Over many years of practice with families and my own experience of parenting, I have concluded that love is not, in fact, enough to make you a good parent. I have seen many parents, who without doubt have loved and adored their children, have their children taken out of their care by local authorities. This is, of course, extremely sad but parents who love their children don't necessarily help them to develop in a healthy or psychologically coherent way and may take their eye off the task sufficiently that their children are in danger or lose out and are disadvantaged. Conversely, I have met parents who have everything imaginable in their lives in terms of privilege, financial security and status, but this is not the same as offering love and good parenting, and so their children still lose out in terms of feeling secure and loved, despite all these other resources. There are many parents who have very little materially but are able to provide secure and commendable parenting to their children so that they grow up to seek advantageous opportunities.

So what are the forces at work that guide parents down the right or wrong road and what are the goals we are heading for? This book is designed to reframe the task and move the parenting game forward so that you understand these forces that are at work and so they are not a mystery to you.

While I don't want to prescribe a framework, I have put together a set of principles and concepts that I have learnt are of importance to the task. These principles and concepts could be broadly termed as leading to 'mindful' or 'mind-minded' parenting that is focused on the developing mind of the child and can be corralled under the term 'Mind Kind'. I want parents to learn the skill of being kind to their child's mind. While I have no intention of starting a trend in parenting, I intend to make it easy for you to think about these things and have developed the acronym of PATACCAKE, which describes the desirable emotional/feeling states or qualities in parents (rather than a desirable set of prescribed behaviours) that combine to make for Mind Kind parenting. PATACCAKE stands for:

Patience

Acceptance

Tolerance

Attunement

Commitment

Compassion

Awareness

Kindness

Empathy.

We can't come up with these constructive emotions and states of mind all the time and we are going to have days when we can only just get through living in an accepting way. We all have to live with our reactive emotions and soothe them as best we can, and really, what would life be if we did not have this reactivity to deal with, and how would we teach our children? Polarity is very much part of the world in which we live. But PATACCAKE is a reminder of where we can be, what is hopeful and as an ideal to aim for when we can. Make a note and stick it on the fridge — PATTACAKE.

Sesame seed

I have also built the acronym SESAME SEED as a way of organizing and grouping together the themes of the material presented in the book. The themes of 'sesame seed parenting' form the cornerstones of being a Mind Kind parent and offer the major clues to achieving parenting that makes your children feel good.

Secure

Secure parenting can be achieved by parents who want to know how to support children to feel stable, secure and able to cope with life. This means the child feels good from the inside because they acknowledge their emotional life, including thoughts, feelings and emotions. They will also have some sense of how to organize, manage and regulate these very real forces that flow through their lives for the rest of their lives. Thoughts and feelings affect behaviour and wellbeing, and they represent the workings of our mind. This means that by paying attention to the inner world of children as well as the outer world, parents are offering enduring skills and support through their relationship with their children.

Emotion

This book looks at the neuroscientific reality that our emotional lives deeply influence our mind, brain and wellbeing and are a force for survival and contentment rather than an annoying human tendency to be ignored. Emotions are a communication to us about our sensory response to our environment, our experience of it and our security within that environment. Parents who are mindful of emotion will help their children experience the broad range of their emotional lives and manage these emotions as a flow of energy and information about themselves, their relationships and their environment. Emotions can range from the depths of despair to the heights of joy and we are made to travel through this range, rather than get stuck in one predominant state.

If we can help our children to understand that minds can change, and to be patient with moods and tolerate uncomfortable states of mind, we will be truly helping them to successfully survive.

Symbolic behaviour

All behaviour is a communication about life and a set of symptoms of what is going on for a child in their environment, and their thoughts and feelings about this. We have to help our children become aware of and manage their own behaviour and channel into positive outcomes the natural energetic impulses that are part of life.

Most behaviour relates to human need. Therefore, behaviour is likely to be a map of our child's needs. If we don't like it we shouldn't blame them for it. Instead, we should look at why it is happening and what we can do to change that. We could remember the five basic needs proposed by William Glasser when he developed 'Reality Therapy' to help young people with dysfunctional behaviour: the need to belong, the need to achieve, the need for fun and enjoyment, the need for freedom and independence and the need to have a sense that we will safely survive.[1] If parents are not fulfilling the totality of these needs, their children will act this out. Reality Therapy viewed human behaviour as goal-orientated and directed at meeting needs. Thus we need to learn the craft of understanding emotion, thought and behaviour.

Adversity

Chapter 4 discusses the fact that life is never going to be without challenge or change. You have to be prepared for periods of adversity and 'mend the roof while the sun is shining'. This means that parents have a grip on the realities of life and are prepared for how to cope when children need more of their help than usual.

It is a certainty that life is going to happen to you, just as it does to every other parent around the world. The cycle of life, death and birth, growth and regrowth is just about the only reliable cycle that we can be sure of and is far more enduring than economic or fashion fads or any other changing system in our fast-paced world. So it is not a case of *if* you will meet something difficult in your life but *when*, whether it is death, loss of a job or something far more unpredictable like a natural disaster, war or illness. Throughout the book I hope you will find resources for how to build a life that gives children the ability to manage adversity. While we face up to how difficult life can be, we also face up to how resourceful we can be as humans and what we can do when the going gets tough. There are few magical solutions, but we can put in imagination and effort to finding real solutions.

Mindfulness and mental health

Mental wellbeing for children could be described as helping them to organize their minds, along with organizing your mind. You will be making that journey to recovery with your child. Your reaction and response to any condition is going to contribute to their recovery. They will need you to feel stable, informed and sure-footed. They don't need your anxiety about them to be added into the mix. It is hard for loving and committed parents not to feel panicky about their children at times — this is only natural. We need to attend to our fears and then move forward. Parents and carers need to understand what is happening in their own mind so that they can support their children from a position of strength and security.

Errors in parenting

You will make errors in your parenting. Chapter 5 shows you that it is not so much the error that you make but the way you put it right that will mean something to your child. So after you shout and overreact (which we have all done) try to understand the situation and talk with your child about it, explaining your reaction and setting out a new plan for a better result next time — both in you and in your child. The key message in Chapter 5 is that children usually make errors by mistake and even if they make them on purpose, we might like to think about why this was done. Every error has some meaning both for you and them — the meaning is that we are learning.

Sense of self and self-image

Regardless of the society we live in, image is important. Archaeology is constantly proving to us that men and women in ancient civilizations (Egypt, for example, some 4000 years ago) were just as focused on what they looked like, as well as what they felt like, spending time on artefacts for themselves and their environments, using make-up and painting their experiences in their homes and temples. It is our creative and social instincts that make us focus on how we choose to present ourselves, but there are psychological issues in play because our self-image is based on our sense of self and how we feel we are accepted within society. We expect teenagers to experiment with self-image while deciding who they are and how they want to be, and we may be surprised at who they want to be.

Eating and self-worth

Ultimately you and your children will become what you eat. You have to decide whether you want to feel like a sugar-coated dough monster or a vibrant vegetable or fruit creature. Or maybe somewhere in between, because there is nothing in the science of eating that says you cannot have any sugar or carbohydrate — far from it. However, it is preferable to derive these substances from natural foods. It is almost certain that you will feel like what you eat and that you will eat in a way that is complementary to how you feel. Chapter 7 takes into consideration the idea of food as a source of emotion and love and talks about our relationship with food as a metaphor for our relationship with ourselves. It discusses children putting on weight and getting too thin. It has been designed to help you through the minefield of feeding children and helping them to feel good about themselves and their growing bodies.

Empathy

Throughout this book you will find the continuous thread of advice on the use of empathy as a tool for understanding your children. Empathy might be the nearest substance to magic fairy dust that we humans have. You will have to decide by practice what you think. Empathic responses, rather than immediate reactions, will tell children that you are at least trying to understand them and willing to work with them.

Every child and human needs empathy, from when they are the tiniest one-hour-old newborn. In this book it emerges as the base for your parenting and love for your children.

Development

Childhood is a journey rather than a destination and children are always travelling in themselves as they grow and develop. It is probably one of the most miraculous things to watch as your children grow, but it is also quite subtle, and some parents find this threatening and don't want their children to explore new pathways of being themselves as their minds develop. It can be confusing as children change dramatically in their outlook and behaviours or it can be a joyful dance to celebrate life — and in reality will probably be a mixture of both. It helps to inform yourself of some of the expected milestones of development so that you can at least have a map of the journey that is being taken and be prepared.

If you have no intention of reading any further than this, then take forward the idea that the most important thing we can be to our children (or anybody else's children) is kind. The term 'mind-minded parenting' tells us to think of the child's mind as we watch them grow. Always try to think about their developing mind and their developing sense of themselves. Minds grow best in positive emotional environments where children feel understood.

If there is one idea to take away it is that whether your children are being really naughty or really perfect, whether they are very settled or quite disturbed, at all times they need your attention and your kind attention to the detail of their lives. Being cruel, angry or frustrated with your children will never help them to learn and never help them to alter their behaviour. You have to learn to be kind to their developing mind — Mind Kind — and to do this you are also going to have to learn to be kinder to yourself. You cannot give to your children what you have not got inside. This includes the principles of sesame seed thinking combined with qualities of that lovely childhood nursery rhyme PATACCAKE. We can bring PATACCAKE qualities to mind any time we choose. Instead of coming at a child with frustration and rage we could stop to think PATACCAKE. I hope you enjoy learning about these qualities in this book. You can follow any framework or structure of parenting, but without these innate universally positive qualities flowing in the environment of your child's life they will not thrive and — in my view — nor will humankind.

When a parent asked me recently if I could give them a good piece of advice about parenting I told them, 'Make the most of every minute with your child'. I hope the style of thinking in this book can help you to make the most of every minute with your precious child or children, whatever your circumstances.

Secure children

As parents we are led to believe in goals for children that, to us, can be confusing. In turn it is likely that we confuse our children. For example, the idea that children must conform to a standard of learning and a set curriculum is an honorable goal, but there is so much more to learn about life and how we are as individuals that cannot be found in these set subjects. Then children quickly realize that they must also conform to certain norms within their social grouping. This is only natural as we are essentially social animals who will learn from one another, and children are brilliant at catching on to trends that maximize their security within a group. But we have to stop and ask ourselves: what are these norms and trends that are being set and are they serving the wellbeing of our children?

Parents, too, start to become anxious if their children do not conform to these standards because parents instinctively know that a child's social survival is very important. Thus to some extent we might be 'buying' security for a child by getting the latest and trendiest object available, from designer labels to smartphones, in order to keep them within their social grouping. Then we start to abide by trends — we're taught, and have it impressed upon us, that our children must have enough exercise, they must not watch too much TV, we must spend time with them, we must not let them eat the wrong thing, we must not let them watch the wrong thing, we must watch for health alerts and so on. Some of these demands are real in certain measure, but are they the real goals of parenting a child or are they just small stops on the way to something much bigger?

My conclusion is that they are secondary goals and that we are not paying enough attention to the primary goals of childhood. The outcome is that parents are very anxious about getting their child the 'right thing' rather than attending to the 'right state of mind'. Are you the kind of parent who gets everything for your child and yet feels dismayed when they still do not appear to be happy? If you are, then you could have the beginnings of insecurity growing in your family, and in yourself, about life and so this chapter may be of help to you. Here I aim to sort out the real issues for you — to give you information based on children's real developmental needs and what truly makes children feel secure from the inside out. Once you have that information you can decide for yourself where you think your parenting might need to develop or where you might need to get help if necessary. You will, of course, continue to help your child conform to social norms and trends, but you will do this from a more secure position knowing that you have attended to the real priorities. You will have more choice about the other things and so will your children.

Psychological security

You might be looking in all directions to see what you need to do or what to get your child next. Here is the good news for you (or possibly the bad news): the primary need of your child is that you feel okay and in a good state of readiness to cope with their lives as well as your own. It all stems from that one fact. To be a good parent, giving it all, you need to take care of your needs — and this does not mean your own designer outfits and being thin enough or rich enough. The thing that children want to feel most in life is that their parents feel secure and safe when they are with them and that this feeling then transfers to them. This is called a 'felt sense' and is also known as psychological security. With a felt sense of security, a child will have a pervasive feeling that their world is going to be held together and managed, in a fashion that keeps them safe and well, and that they can get on with the task of exploring life and relationships. This is what your children really want from you. They might think they need lots of other things like computer games and the latest toy, and of course it might help them if they do have these things in their lives. I cannot dismiss the fact that toys are extremely appealing to children, though the vital truth is that they can grow and develop quite well without these things, but they will not grow and develop without learning from you or without a felt sense that you are coping and that life is a safe place to be. So many of the children I have met in mental health services are mildly to moderately troubled because they feel they have had no psychological anchor onto which they can hold during their episode of difficulty.

This throws the ball back into your court but is not intended to be a parent-blaming exercise. It is intended to help you to look in the right direction. In later chapters I will tell you more about developing your own felt sense of security and developing yourself. In this chapter, though, I will focus on children.

Let's take children who are school aged and beyond. What is it that happens to children who live with a felt sense of security? What can we expect to see? Will they be brilliant at their school work, get picked first for sports teams and get a first class degree at university or have a brilliant career as a wealthy entrepreneur? Possibly not. But they will have certain psychological capabilities that will enhance their lives, and you have to ask yourself how much you value these capabilities.

Much of the excellent material that I have drawn on in this chapter comes from Professor Peter Fonagy's research for his work, 'Attachment representations in school-age children: The development of the child attachment interview'.[1] Here, he focused on trying to assess a child's value system with regard to their attachment or relationship style with their parent, as he knew from experts that it was so important to the wellbeing of children, the work of John Bowlby being the origins of the description of this attachment process.[2]

The psychological capabilities of children who live with a felt sense of security might include the following.

They will feel that the world is a good enough place to be

Children don't go around being excited if the world feels like a good place to be, but they do show us that they feel safe and that they can explore their environment and get on with learning, and that is exciting to them. This overriding sense that it's good to be alive is the richest of human resources, and it is a great achievement if we can raise children who wake each morning with the felt sense that today will be a great day because there are people on whom they can rely.

Psychological security won't stop difficult things from happening, and it does not mean they will have perfect lives. It does mean, though, that they are resourced with psychological patterns of behaviour that lead them, on the whole, to believe that they can manage and that if they cannot manage then they can find someone who can. A perfectly happy and secure child can come across challenging experiences and at these times they need to feel that someone is there to protect them and feel their feelings with them. They might be bullied at school, for example, and this is a worst-case scenario for any child unless they have a parent who can sort it out very quickly for them. They may get ill, they may even get very ill or become disabled. Nothing can stop these things from happening, but if they have a fundamental sense that they will be as supported as possible then this is the baseline for a positive and hopeful life. It is the trampoline from which children can launch themselves into daily experience and is the basis of real happiness.

When I trained in attachment theory, I often told a true story about a child in very real difficulty. A family living near the sea owned a boat and they frequently went out with their happy group of children, one of whom was their twelve-year-old daughter. The family were sleeping in the boat one night far out at sea when their daughter sleepwalked over the side while the rest of the family stayed asleep. When the family woke up in the morning she was nowhere to be found and there could only be one answer as to where she was — somewhere at sea. Fortunately, these parents had put their children to sleep in their life jackets. Air and sea rescue were called immediately and the area was searched. Twelve hours later the young girl was found shaken but not stirred, just a little sunburnt and hungry. When this child was interviewed she was asked what she had thought when she woke up and found that she was floating at sea on her own. She said, 'I knew my dad would look for me.' This thought was the child's psychological life jacket and this is what a felt sense of security means. It's automatic.

They will be able to distinguish positive from negative

Children who have a felt sense of security will feel safe enough to comment on their world and evaluate it in a realistic way. (This refers to children from the age of seven, as younger children do not have the brain development for this capability and we cannot expect it of them.) They will be able to evaluate their parents' state of mind as well as comment on their own, and will be able to say things like 'My dad's not very good at mending the car so he couldn't fix it and we were late for school', and express frustration and disappointment about this. At the same time, the same child would be able to look at what their father gets right — 'He helps me with my homework.' They will be able to comment, 'Mum is a bit upset today; that makes me feel sad too, but she says she will feel better soon.'

Essentially, secure children feel they have permission to comment on life as they see it without judgmental responses from defensive parents. If we extend this into children's lives as a whole we will be able to see that, if they comment on what they find difficult, there is more likelihood that they will be able to gain help at these times in their lives. So when a child says,

'I don't like this', the parent might not be able to change anything, but it becomes a matter for parental attention to which they try to give meaning.

This kind of emotional literacy relating to good and bad gives a child a way to describe their experience and help others understand them. The child feels that their conversation is worthy of attention and they will bother to make a narrative about life because life is full of good and bad things that are interesting. It is far healthier to have children who can talk about how life is for them, even if it does take up more parental time and give parents something to think about themselves. What more can a parent do than share a child's experience and information about that experience when they are asked, and then respond accordingly? This very simple parental behaviour is the one you need to hold in mind if you want your child to feel a sense of security.

They will label and express emotions

There are many reasons why emotional literacy is so vital to our existence. Essentially, our emotions help us to understand where we are inside ourselves and there are plenty of reasons why we should not ignore these communications. Children being emotional is to be expected and respected, and is worthy of our attention rather than being viewed as an inconvenient aspect of childhood that makes us cross. A child being emotional is as natural as a puppy biting your hand, because that is instinctive — the puppy is not being naughty, it is just behaving instinctively. Children are born to communicate through emotions and use sound so that they draw our attention to themselves. Eventually the sound of those emotions will become communication and a narrative (or set of words) on life. When we accept the sounds of childhood as vital to their lives and wellbeing, we accept children as they are and they, again, have that felt sense of us being there for them.

They will feel accepted

A sense of acceptance is big currency in life. It is worth more than money. A sense of acceptance and belonging in our primary family of care (or adopted or substitute family or care group) is the deepest gift on offer in this lifetime and nothing can replace the sense of wellbeing or contentment that this will give to children.

The quality of acceptance for children can be found within the heart of the key adults in their lives (including teachers and professionals). It is another of those enriching commodities in life that is totally free, and when children receive this gift they learn self-acceptance.

The opposite of acceptance is rejection, and if you have lived with even minor rejection you know how painful this feels and how it disturbs your sense of wellbeing, affecting your ability to think clearly. It is very easy, in the present day, to think we are giving children a sense of acceptance by giving them a material need, when in fact we could be doing exactly the opposite if we think that objects will replace our presence and emotional availability to our children.

This starts to tell us something about our positioning on what children really want. They really want to feel we have time for them, that we can hear them, receive their communications and make sense of them. Ultimately, many parents are frustrated that they cannot seem to pacify their children and that their children always want something from them, yet they do not notice how they have, in fact, set themselves up to fail. It is true that children do always want something but that something is you, their primary parent. (When I use the term parent in this book I refer to the whole variety of parents and carers that are available to children, so please count yourself in whether you are a foster carer, single parent, adoptive parent, parent who does not live with a child, step-parent or even parent of a child who is grown up — the term is not meant to be exclusive.) These opportunities to feel connected to a caregiver are the currency and material of parenting relationships; they are great riches that poverty or adversity simply cannot wear away.

They will have a coherent self

Coherence in self really refers to the way we experience ourselves as well as the way others experience us. A dictionary definition refers to 'a state of logical or orderly relationship of parts', and since we are made of many parts it is always reassuring that those pull together to work as a coherent whole. You could think of this as all the parts of an engine running smoothly due to the use of the right oil. As a body, a mind and a self, living in a world depending on our relationships, we need to be able to rely on ourselves working in a coherent and orderly fashion. At times, when people notice that we are incoherent, we would hope that we might rely on them to help us out, assuming that they love and care enough about us to do so.

A typical example of this would be when children are ill. If you've noticed what happens you'll see their little show fall off the rails and they cannot hold onto their self-organizing skills. You have probably noticed that the same happens to you: everything that was easy when you were well is so difficult when you are ill. With children, for a few days before you realize they are ill you might be baffled by their behaviour. Then suddenly their temperature breaks out and they collapse into a heap and need to be cared for while the body restores itself. Once all is well and restoration is in place the mind can light up again and begin to behave in an organized way. Your child can cope again. Perhaps you will have noticed this in yourself at times of adversity. Fortunately, our brains are very well adjusted to cope with these times under normal circumstances. Just let it all fall to pieces and it will all come back together again when you are restored and feeling well enough.

During times of mental health difficulties or adversity, adults and children need real support so they know that people care, which dramatically affects their chances of recovery. Thus, children who have had support from their parents over the small things in life will be able to face adversity as it comes with this natural sense that they can cope. They will have a sense that their brain and mind will return to a functioning version of themselves in due course, even after things have been difficult. This is what brains like to do — they prefer to be functioning well and harmoniously, and are always working towards this goal.

This is what coherence of mind means: pulling things back together so that normal brain functioning can continue for our wellbeing. So coherence is an important word when we are thinking about the care of children. You don't have to be perfect as a parent, but you do have to try to be as coherent and as organized, functional and meaningful in your behaviours as you can be. The more children have the sense that their small emerging mind and self has the support and attention they need, the more they will enjoy being alive with an inherent sense that all chaos can be restored, rather than life being a self-defeating and incoherent package of meaningless and unconnected events.

If you are not sure about this, here is a simple test. Take a look at how you are as a person. Take a look around your house: is there a comfortable sense of organization or is it a disaster area for yourself and your family? Do you feel like you are managing the physical environment of your home or is it managing you? Are you constantly firefighting the chaos? Does the environment represent the coherence in your own mind or does it represent some other state of mind to which you have not attended? You could then ask your children to look around their own rooms. Ask them what the state of their own room says about themselves? Your environment is a direct representation of yourself and your mind. Is it organized enough to make life easier?

They will be alert to information about relationships

At an instinctive level we are all alert to information about relationships. What does this mean to us? In the rush of our everyday lives, along with our bid to cope and survive, be more effective and hold a family together, parents may forget the underlying basis of relationships. We are so engrossed in the 'have to', 'musts' and 'shoulds' that we can forget to give meaning to the basis of relationships. This is not surprising, as we live in an age of exceptional alertness to image and communication, but not necessarily exceptional alertness to relationships. So what does this mean for us? You might be baffled by what your children need, or wondering why they are so discontented. You may feel worn out by trying to give your children everything, only to find that they still want something else.

There are some rules to the basics here. When your baby was born, or when the child you care for was born, they will have searched through the shapes that surrounded them and found one thing upon which their eyes could rest and provoke their curiosity. That one thing was your face, and from that very moment your baby began learning about all the information in your face, about you and about the things going on around you, bearing in mind that in the womb you don't get to see many faces (even if you are a twin). This is the child's instinctive survival technique at work. In turn, parents search their child's face to understand how they are and who they are because faces are an important register of how we are, both inside and out. This behaviour occurs in varying degrees and patterns, so don't worry if your baby closed their eyes and went to sleep having seen your face. While babies are born to connect with you, we have understood for some time that the way that they connect varies according to their birth temperament.[3] They may be an easy baby or a fractious baby but this doesn't matter; it's all behaviour to survive combined with their inherited temperament and it's all there for a parent or carer to interpret and cope with.

This is the start of a basic question in life: how are you and how does it show?

they connect varies according to their birth temperament.[3] They may be an easy baby or a fractious baby but this doesn't matter; it's all behaviour to survive combined with their inherited temperament and it's all there for a parent or carer to interpret and cope with.

Our children continue to use faces as sources of this information but of course they forget that they are using faces and they just get on with making friends (or falling out sometimes) and exploring and creating in their world. The degree to which they are interested in relationships depends very much on their temperament at birth and the way in which they have been taught to be curious about others. But, to whatever extent one is curious and fascinated by the signpost of the face, what is true is that reading social signals is an essential part of our survival. Thus, children who don't read social signals very well, either in people's faces or expressions of emotion, are chronically disadvantaged and find themselves in difficult social positions. This is particularly true of children with autism, in which reading signals from others is very low on their inherited agenda. In these sorts of cases we have to help children to read signals as best they can and give them a lot of support and guidance on the issue of norms and appropriate communication. This is, of course, exceedingly demanding on a parent in this situation but many children with autism can have a secure sense of parenting with the right input.

Secure children without autism may adopt the sense from their parents that this is a meaningful thing to do rather than just a waste of time. Thus, they feel a sense of conviction that it matters to notice others and what they might be thinking, and, like anything to which we give our attention, the more we give our focus to it the more we are likely to become an expert at it. The more adept we are at reading social cues through reading people's faces and body language, the more we are likely to get social cues correct and respond in the right way. Secure children will never go around thinking, 'Lucky me, I got top marks in reading faces' — they will thankfully take this for granted and get on with their busy lives, using this information to keep them in relationships.

Raising secure children should not become another matter for parents to get anxious about, nor is there a need to find classes for your kids in 'reading the face'. It does not mean that parents who have forgotten to do this, who did not realize it was important or did not have the advantage themselves of parents who helped them feel secure, are going to be the losers. We can all help people to notice and read the signs of one another if we just take the time to notice and respond. Teachers will help children in their school environment and children will learn from others what they need to know. If nothing else, I think it is helpful that parents should know that below the surface there is some busy activity going on around being alert to relationships. Your child will be reading your face — are you reading theirs?

They will be angry and frustrated at times but will be able to manage this and rely on you

If you are available to deal with your child's issues as they arise, it is highly likely that by the time they are adults they will have absorbed the tendency to deal with issues more effectively, having received all of your help. There are issues and there are big issues, and secure parents will have a sense that issues fall into categories. First there are the issues such as 'I can't find my PE shorts'. These are practical issues in which a child can learn, with your help, about keeping their things in some kind of order. There is no point in getting cross with a child because they cannot organize their PE shorts — they don't have good memories until they are around ten years old and even then they won't remember everything. The second category includes the things that you just have to organize, such as the structure of their day and the way their time runs, the issue of routine and organization. This is entirely your domain and responsibility, although a child between five and ten could have some input into this and you can help them learn to plan.

The third set of priorities includes attention to their inner life and information from their thoughts, feelings and emotions. This involves you listening as well as noticing their behaviour as both of these are sources of good information about children. If your child is upset, it is because they are upset about something important to them, not because they wish to annoy you. If your child is angry it is because they are angry about something important, not just because they like being angry. It is up to you to put in some time to consider these communications and help them out. A basic rule, then, is that a child cannot sort out their own emotional life and they will need your help with this. It is not okay to leave them to cope on their own.

As you build these patterns of continual behaviour with your child by dealing with their small problems, you can be pleased that you are fulfilling a long-term goal of helping them towards autonomy and secure independence. Children do not just do this on their own. You are also helping them to deal with both practical and emotional issues and not stay stuck with frustration or anger. There are two things children can do when their parents are not helping them to cope. They can get quieter about it and not bother to ask any more, or they can get noisier about it and continue to be a child preoccupied with troubled thoughts and emotions. The easiest way to prevent this is to attend to it in the here and now so that your child has a good balance between these two positions, which is the secure approach. Children who tone down their emotions so drastically that they don't bother any more will develop personalities around this kind of response (these are often known in psychology as an avoidant pattern of behaviour).[4] Unfortunately, if we do not continually teach children to problem-solve and support their learning, these problems can then develop into big problems.

So if we are in parenting for the long game we want to think about attending to those issues now (within reason). You are only human and you cannot do it all right now but you can let your children know, 'I will be with you as soon as I can on that — it's important to me.' Let them know your intention is to help them.

It does not matter if you did not have the perfect experience of being parented yourself. You can live and learn behaviours from others. One of the parents whom I have supported has allowed me to reproduce her thoughts on learning to parent to help her child feel more secure.

Notes from a parent with an insecure childhood

When I was a child I used to notice how parents used to talk with their children. By the time I was a teenager I noticed that some parents talked more to their kids than others. I was particularly interested in the way that my best friend's mum was very interested in her life — that was so fascinating to me and somehow made me feel good inside. It also made me feel good that her mother paid attention to her friends (i.e. me). She used to say positive things to me and I felt great.

Notes from the same parent who learnt about parenting

When I first became a parent, I remembered the style of parenting that I saw in my friends' parents and the way they related to their children. I learnt from others that it was okay to be sensitive and supportive and interested. Sometimes I was unsure of myself as to what this meant, as it was not embedded so comfortably in my memory. Sometimes I was switched off, thinking that babies could manage on their own, but then my baby would cry so much that I would think there must be something I had to do. Eventually my baby taught me to respond to her. She had a training plan for me.

Parenting today

In this chapter we have been looking at what we know about children who experience security as a felt sense. This means that it is embedded in their very nervous system. It does not mean that life is going to be perfect; rather that they have a rich inner resource and a platform with which to face our complex world. There are few scientists or researchers who would disagree with the idea that a parent's support for a child is the basis of them feeling well and happy. There is some disagreement about how much this is to do with parental interaction with a child or whether this is led by the child's temperament at birth or their learning in the social world. Let's be moderate in our approach — it is very likely to be a mixture of both. The idea that a parent has to respond and be sensitive to a baby in infancy is probably by now irrefutable and has been proven many times over by science and research in fields ranging from anthropology to psychology and evolutionary science. You do have to be interested and you do have to be there, or you do have to have someone there who will substitute for you and be similarly sensitive and committed to your baby.

Realistically, many parents today struggle between the call of their infant and the demands of keeping a roof over the head of their family, and this raises issues of what parents do with their children when they are working. I know it raises a whole set of issues of how parents and carers feel about how they are pressured into separation from their children. Busy working parents can be compromised in the security they can give their children simply because they are not present. I know that it is not the parents' fault that they have to work. I had to work when I raised my daughter and stepson and frequently felt compromised in caring for them. I had to find other people to do the job for me. Anyone who cares for our children has to be committed to spend time with them and have their mind on them in a sensitive and thoughtful way. It would of course be ideal if that person was you, because you have their best interests at heart all the time. But that is just not always possible.

Of equal value in terms of care is a substitute person whom you know can be sensitive and thoughtful to your child, anyone ranging from a relative to a childminder. It does not matter so much 'who' but 'how' they do this. As a concerned parent you will choose someone who is safe, kind and caring. Your child is a part of you, not a commodity to be passed around and if you feel happy about their care when you are away from them, it is likely you will be less fretful, too, in the times when you are with them.

This year I worked with a parent who talked to me about her son who was anxious and feeling suicidal. She had no idea whatsoever about how to conceive of his problems. After a small amount of time spent helping her to understand some of the above issues about her relationship with her child, she stopped her high-powered job that brought in a large salary as she realized her son needed her at home. He quickly recovered. Another parent in a similar situation, with a child who was self-harming and feeling suicidal with anorexia, did not feel able to give up her job but she did take a month off from work to give time to her child's issues rather than managing them from her desk. That total focus and a willingness to think about her child's anxiety was enough to resolve these quite serious mental health issues. In each case, and in many other cases where children recover, I have seen a willingness by the parent to let go and try a new pattern of behaviour. This approach meant that they gave themselves more time to give their child more time. Ultimately, this was all that was needed and the solution really did lie within the parent making that decision.

▲▲▲

In conclusion

Children are primed and programmed to demand more and more from us and you might need help to identify the organic needs of the child that must be met if they are to feel secure from the inside. It is safe to say no to a child if they ask for the latest thing that they feel they need, but it is not safe to take your eye off their need for you to protect them and prioritize their care. As we have seen, secure kids express emotions, talk about negative as well as positive experiences and feel they have the right to comment on their lives. They will have problems and they will bring you those problems if they are secure. There is no way out of having problems in life when you are a child. Your real hope lies in a thoughtful parent who is sensitive to what is worrying you, who takes your issues seriously and realizes that what you really need is them and their mind working for you.

Finally

» What your child really needs is you and your attention. There is nothing on this planet you can buy that will replace that.

» Emotions are beautiful aspects of our humanity that keep us informed about the state of our children and ourselves.

» If you put effort into anything, put it into helping your child feel loved, safe and accepted.

» Help your child resolve negative emotions. It is a fantastic way to care for their mental health and make them feel secure. It could be said to be the first building block of good mental health.

» Take note of how important the quality of the relationship is with your child. This is demonstrated by being there for them to deal with the small issues they face on a daily basis.

» Demonstrate coherence and self-organization to your child by pulling your own act together first. What emotional state are you demonstrating to your child?

» If you can't be there then find a sensitive, safe and thoughtful person who can fill this role. Try not to fret over being pulled in different directions over work, income and responsibility to your child. Put your child first by ensuring good quality childcare.

Emotion before thought

In this chapter we will explore the very sound reasons why listening to your child's emotions will enhance their wellbeing, support their development and make them happier and more confident. You may have been raised with many myths about your emotional life. Here are some facts.

Emotions are a primitive form of communication, a connection between the brain and the body. The brain is fed by information from our sensory system and this is translated into mental and emotional material. Traditionally we might think of five senses — sight, sound, taste, touch and smell. But the whole body is in fact a sensory system and we are constantly experiencing life with and through our bodies.

One of the focuses of this book is to help parents understand that we are both mammals as well as incredibly refined human beings with highly evolved brains. Many parents are baffled by parenting young children because they have not been taught to make this strong link between the two aspects of our selves. When babies are born they are little mammals waiting to develop into human beings with more sophisticated thinking brains, but their relational brain is ready and working when they are born. This means they want to be in a relationship with someone so that they survive, and they are programmed to achieve this goal. We have already established that as soon as babies are born this relational brain begins to work and the focus begins on the faces that babies see, the things they hear and, of vital importance initially, the way they are touched, soothed and held. Information is also given to their relational brain by the way they are fed, the way they are spoken to, the vibration of the voice, the way they are protected and cared for by you, and the warmth and sensitivity they are shown. Parents and carers, whoever they are, immediately become aware of this intense need for sensitivity in response to a newborn. Very few people think it's a good idea to behave in a harsh way in the presence of a newborn baby.

The relational brain is the older part of our brain, which developed long before our cognitive and thinking brain. It had all the equipment we needed to help us survive a primitive environment. It helped us to run if there was danger and to fight if we needed to. Gradually, as we evolved, we began to learn that working with others helped humankind to survive and this ancient story of our development is mirrored in the growth process we see in every single child. A child is born with that early brain active and ready for relationship action. The infant clings, snuggles and calls for attention and manages to make adults alert to his or her needs. Over the next five years of the child's life the brain develops and the frontal part, the cognitive (thinking) system, becomes active. This is a gradual process, not an overnight occurrence. We know when children have arrived at this stage of cognitive activity because they start to ask questions and use words as a marker of all that they see around them. Mostly they ask the question, 'Why?' This is because their brain is very busy thinking about the world that they see or feel. They also realize that everything in the world has a name attached to it as they begin to find language and this is why you will be frequently confronted with the question 'why?' Don't ever be annoyed by this question — it's such a gift from your child, whose brain is developing before your eyes. Some parents will be aware of this and excited by it, whereas other might dismiss this evolution of their child and take it for granted. This highlights an important distinction that I am drawing between being mind aware, or Mind Kind, and mind unaware, which I call Mind Blind.

In many ways our emotional system could be referred to as the child inside ourselves that needs our regular attention. In fact, many styles and models of therapy have referred to the child inside ourselves and the ability to pay attention to that. One of these models is transactional analysis, as developed by Eric Berne.[1]

Transactional analysis is a fancy name for a very simple model that helps us to think about the brain. Berne found a brilliant way to communicate this information to people by telling them that their mind has the capacity to be both an adult logical thinker as well as an emotional child. At the same time, he noted the capacity of the mind to hold on to our values and rules in life regarding the things we should, must and ought to do in order to survive. In our world we are most concerned with what we have to do to survive socially. It has become as important to us as avoiding sabre-toothed tigers was to ancient humans. Berne proposed three aspects of our brain, just as Freud had done, but he tried to make Freud's model more accessible. As adults we can hopefully move around all these aspects of our mind. What we have to remember if we are mind aware is that children have limited capacity to be logical, depending on their stage of development. Thus, when I had a mother suggest that her two-year-old had no capacity for anger management, it was not hard to see that she needed a lot of help from me to understand that, so that she could give her beautiful toddler a chance.

Another important thing to remember about emotion is that we affect each other with emotions. If we have an emotional state it is likely that it will affect others who are in our near vicinity, especially those who are close to us and feel for us. This is a fundamental rule that seems to get forgotten in our busy, information-based world. We forget to use emotional information and we forget that it affects us all, especially those who are close to us, including our children. Our primitive communication may be ancient but it is remarkably intelligent. These systems have developed so that we are made to read each other at a sensory and then an affective level. This is a fact, it is happening right now as you read these words. Just put down the book for a moment and notice how you are 'affected' by these words and let that idea sink in for a while. What emotion arises for you in the present moment?

So how does this relate to parenting skills? It points to a very important fact: how you are in your affective state is how your child experiences you. So, in fact, infants might experience you more acutely than anybody else around you. They may sense anxiety, fear or stress and they will certainly sense depression and negative emotions such as hostility, rage and disgust, and they may very easily feel that it is part of them.

Here is the rule: **whatever is going on for you is likely to affect your child**.

Naming, reclaiming and understanding emotions

One of the biggest parenting mistakes that I observe is misreading children's emotional states. It is *the* major parenting mistake in my view, and it is so easy to put right with just a little understanding.

You are the bigger person with the bigger brain

You are the one responsible for first seeking to understand. It puts impossible and very distressing pressure onto children if they have to allow for the emotional lives of their parents all the time and are not having their own understood. You must prioritize your child's need for parenting before your own. So when your child is in an emotional state, the very last thing you need to do is react, and the very first thing you need to do is stop and think for a moment about what is going on for your child.

You don't have to know immediately; you just have to stop, listen and respond in a kind way. This is Mind Kind.

Children need help with their emotional states

From birth until adulthood (and beyond, as parents with grown-up children will know) children need support with regulating and making sense of their emotions. They need you there to first soothe and then to make sense of their emotions. So children require a two-step plan: soothe and understand. Not 'get mad and dismiss', not 'go hysterical because you are having a bad day', not 'ignore and hope it will go away', but pay attention, help to soothe and then seek to put words and understanding to the emotion.

Some parents are fearful that their children will not become independent as soon as possible and learn to deal with themselves and self-manage, so there may be some anxiety that paying attention to the emotional states of their children will make them too soft or that they will not then become autonomous and self-soothing and stand on their own two feet. There is no evidence to suggest that this is the case. However, there is plenty of evidence to suggest that supporting children with their emotions will help them to become emotionally secure, well-balanced individuals. It is no mistake that, in Chapter 1 when we looked at the elements of security in a child, we named emotional literacy and emotional openness as two of these elements. Research by child development expert Alan Sroufe, in his 30-year study of child development from birth to adulthood, found that children who are supported are likely to be more secure.[2]

Another finding, from the work of Professor Peter Fonagy of the Anna Freud Institute and University College London, is the phenomenon of what he refers to as 'Mentalization'.[3] This is the ability to think about the states of mind within ourselves and others, in order to make sense of them. It is our capacity to make sense of our emotional and mental states that identifies our ability to cope and manage in life and is likely to support not only emotional wellbeing but also better outcomes in mental health. (I will talk later about our mental health as an adult.) Mentalization is where we try to think about the states of others as well as ourselves, trying to anticipate what is in the minds of others. This process is a form of Mind Kind but it is also a way of keeping ourselves safe. If we know what is in the mind of another, we know what is likely to happen next in a relationship. Much anxiety centres on trying to read what is in people's minds and much child anxiety is about trying to read what is in the minds of parents — especially if they are troubled. We all mind read to a certain extent and children are trainee mind readers, trying to learn from us.

I would like to make this process as understandable as possible from a parental perspective. So in my own study and research on working with children with complex behavioural difficulties I came to the 5R formula for helping children with complex (or even very ordinary) emotional states, helping to repair their anxiety so that it does not lead to despair. The five Rs were: receive, regulate, resolve, repair and repeat. The 5R formula became 6R formula when one of my students suggested that the sixth R was for routine, which is so important to children. So here is the formula for children who are living relatively normal lives, and are not damaged by neglect of their emotions.

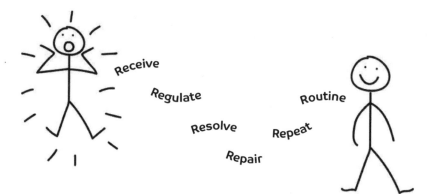

Receive
Regulate
Resolve
Repair
Repeat
Routine

In this model we think of emotions as communications rather than meaningless noise. They are communications coming from the child and directed at you for your attention. The problem for us adults is that exceptionally small things (in our perception) create exceptionally big problems for children. For example, 'Where is my blankey?' followed by an outburst of distress just means yet another task to a parent. To a child it means that something they love and that makes them feel secure, safe and cosy is temporarily out of sight, which has led to anxiety. If we can learn to respect these communications, we are likely to be far happier as parents because we can find resolutions (most of the time) and we are being Mind Kind. Some of the most common parenting errors can be made when parents misread the emotions of children. Nearly as common are the errors made when parents do not respect or address the emotional lives of children.

Acceptance

We are moving into a realm here which can be labelled 'acceptance', where we are close to understanding through accepting what we see in children and not rejecting or dismissing it. We talked about this in the previous chapter, but we were talking about acceptance in relation to making children feel they belong. Now we are talking about acceptance of inner states and we are broadening our minds as to what we will or will not accept — and, of course, we cannot accept in our children's minds that which we are unable to accept in ourselves. Thus, if you reject your own sadness when it arrives in your life, or if you dismiss your own anger when it emerges, it is very likely that you will not be able to accept these emotions in your children and they will not know the healing power or meaning of these emotions in their lives.

Let's look at the emotions we are likely to encounter through being human. In this you will have a chance to identify those emotions that you can accept and those that you cannot accept. You may well ask: what is it that acceptance of emotions does for us? And I think this is worthy of explanation.

Acceptance is an emotional state that brings pacification to the mind and literally regulates our states. If we are mentally fighting or rejecting a concept or experience, we can have no peace and we cannot move forward to the next step that is needed. So, for example, if you are learning something new and this makes you feel anxious, if you can accept that anxiety is a natural part of the learning process, it is likely you will then be able to soothe yourself into a more secure state of mind ready for learning. The state of acceptance makes everything possible — even the very difficult things in life. If a psychological state is worthy of interest and application, it has to be applicable to the gambit of human life, not just the simple things.

One of the big areas of life where acceptance is the key to moving forward is the area of death and loss. If we lose a loved one we very clearly get put into a state of distress, regret, grief and turmoil and this state can continue for some years as you readjust to life without your loved one. The final stage of the grief process is that of acceptance of the loss and the recognition that there is nothing that can be done to fight the inevitability of death or often the circumstances of death. So, in loss, the time of resolution is when acceptance has been achieved. This is a process, it does not all happen at once and, in a way, acceptance of the process is the important point rather than the expectation that you will suddenly arrive at acceptance. All the same, a state of acceptance of things as they are brings us to some sense of completion, resolution and peace of mind, whereas fighting our emotions as they arise costs a lot of energy and simply keeps us stuck.

So, what is it exactly that is presented to us in the emotional lives of children? Let's get down to some of the detail and look at ways to greet these emotions with acceptance rather than rejection. Let's get to know them now so that when they arise next time in yourself you can start to befriend these emotional states rather than reject them.

Anger

If something makes you angry, it is a communication for a reason. It does not mean that you have to act out in a gigantic way — breaking things, shouting and being frightening. It's not good for your relationships to do this, especially with your children and loved ones. A great way to handle anger is to accept and name it, and try to identify what problem has caused you to become distressed and anxious. It is likely that you have something to reorganize or some psychological readjustment to make, perhaps in conjunction with someone. Usually we are angry because we are frustrated in our goals or because we think that something is unjust or unfair and threatens our life.

For example, you're angry because you are stuck in a traffic jam on the motorway. Listen to the communication — the anger is not surprising because your goals have been frustrated and you cannot get to where you were expecting to be. You may even be causing inconvenience or disruption to others. It might be keeping you separate from your loved ones or stopping you in your capacity to earn money so that your family can survive. So what do you do? Continue to be angry and enraged or have a talk with yourself about readjusting that goal? You can't shift the traffic jam so you have to reset your arrangements for the day, adjust your timeframe and so on, so that you regulate your state of arousal. Learn from the experience; next time around don't drive at that time if there is likely to be a jam.

The same applies to our children. Sometimes children can have some very unrealistic goals for themselves and for you. Some of their goals can be achieved and some cannot, and it is up to us as we help our children to grow in life to get them to realize that not all their goals can be achieved at the snap of their fingers. However, we will only achieve this if we help them to understand this process and are deeply sympathetic to the anxiety that they feel when they cannot get what they think they want. It is the way we talk to our children and the narrative we provide on life that will ease them into managing their own anger. So if your child gets angry because they cannot go for a sleepover and all their other friends are going, then we show that you accept their anger. This does not mean that you give in; you just work with them on this. You provide a narrative: 'I understand that you wanted to do that and that you must feel that you are missing out, so you feel angry and a bit worried … you can't go this time because I did not put it in my diary and have made other arrangements, but I absolutely do want you to go to sleepovers and I will make sure I fix the next one in my diary so we can do it. Why not ring your friend and tell them that?'

In this process we are giving our children the most precious gift: not giving in. We are teaching them that life is not always easy, that they cannot have everything they want, that you are not a doormat or a pushover, and that these things can be put right next time around. They also learn that you understand their anger, you accept their emotions and that while emotions do need to be listened to, they also have to be moderated; they don't have to turn into a demand that the child has his or her own way all the time. Finally, they understand that life can be and can feel unfair. This is a reality. The best we can do when we feel something is unfair is discuss this with someone who understands.

Frustration

Don't take frustration away from your children — it is so much a part of learning in life. Children who have low frustration tolerance often also find it hard to learn. Help them with frustration — name it, talk about it, tell them that you feel it, help them to understand what goes on inside themselves and how after frustration they may well make a breakthrough and find a new level of learning. Frustration occurs when we are stopped from reaching the goal we desire, and it leads to anger if we let it. But frustration is also a natural part of learning.

Excessive frustration could suggest we are trying to reach the wrong goal and it can help to evaluate frustration when it arrives in your life. Does it mean 'hang in there' or does it mean 'adjust that goal slightly'? I remember my nine-year-old daughter trying to write a poem for school, getting frustrated and crying when she could not find the words. As I know the experience of writing poetry, I knew this was part of the process so I talked to her and advised her to wait a little longer to see what thoughts she had rather than give in. I told her she could not expect words to be automatic. She did wait, and she did write her poem and has turned into a beautiful writer in her adult years. That, I mainly put down to her ability to tolerate frustration.

Fear

Fear is perhaps the rawest and most primitive emotion that is working for us and for our survival. Therefore, it underlies everything we do and is often the basis of many conflicts, especially when people are not used to listening, moderating, living with and understanding this emotion. Fear that is not managed, heard and understood simply becomes a continuous underlying state of anxiety about life. If one cannot have one's fear attended to and managed, it is suppressed and becomes a general fearful state that is ever present. In fact, what really signifies securely attached children is their ability to moderate and manage their fear. Initially, of course, this is with the help of a supportive adult.

Children are fearful of many things, both real and imagined, and they need help with learning to use logic to check out the reality of their fears. Night-time fears and anxieties are almost obligatory in childhood and unless they are settled and managed with a kindly acceptance they grow into terrors that are disproportionate and simply larger than life. Children are separate from you at night-time, it is dark and they become more vulnerable as they lose consciousness, so there is actually some real basis to this sense of increased vulnerability and fear. In a less evolved world they would be more open to attack and so they need your reassurance to build up their confidence that night-time is safe.

If children express fear about something that is unimaginable to an adult mind, my advice is to first check thoroughly that there is no real basis to this fear. There may be some reality to it somewhere. On the other hand, we do not want to show children that we are worried by their fears and worries; we need to show them that we are confident we can deal with all matters relating to their safety (even if we actually cannot). This is a hard call for parents who are worried about matters of survival themselves (money, relationships, work, etc.) or worse fears such as famine and war, which bring extreme hardship. When parents come under pressure and feel fear about their survival, we know that children quickly mirror that fear back to them, particularly if parents cannot soothe the child's fear, and they become caught in a mutually dysregulating cycle of invisible difficulty.

Parents should take time to reflect on their own fears and evaluate their own inner state and measure the impact this may have on their children. We have to know that children will start hiding their fearful emotions from us if they feel that we cannot handle them.

Joy

Joy is such a good indicator of wellbeing. It is rather tedious if people appear joyful all the time, as it tends to indicate something out of kilter in their thinking or a shallow disposition. Joy can only emerge when children or adults are safe, happy and well. It cannot be present with other negative emotions. We can't be afraid and joyful, we can't be anxious and joyful, and we can't be joyful all the time. Joy surges through us as a result of emotional wellbeing.

Joy is what children experience when their parents are happy and all is well in their world, and when they are close to people they love. If your child is depressed there is an absence of joy in their lives, and with older children you can notice this quite easily. The antidote to depression is to increase a sense of joy, but this cannot be achieved by buying them a new object. It is more likely to be achieved by spending good quality time with your child, engaging in a shared (with each other or in a group) activity or interaction. It could be as simple as playing a board game or sharing a milkshake or a few loving words at bedtime.

Sadness

Sadness, like all other emotions, is a natural response to an event that is upsetting — like the loss of a loved one, a pet or an unexpected change. These things cannot be avoided in any of our lives. Tears and upset will not harm children and all that is needed at sad times is our loving and kind attention combined with reassurance and support.

Sadness can last for days or even weeks and months if children have been bereaved or had a nasty incident. Children need to be observed during these times to see how they are managing, but what is clear is that sadness is a manageable human emotion. Nobody dies from being sad, but people do get very ill and experience depression and anxiety when they repress their sadness and it does not get attention in an appropriate way, when it becomes stuck inside and is not given an outlet or allowed to integrate and be made sense of.

People deal with and process sadness in many different ways. Notably, art and music are very helpful in assisting children to reflect on their sadness, but what is ultimately required is that someone notices and offers to share that experience.

Shame

Shame is our friend too. It is the socializing emotion, part of our evolutionary heritage to ensure maintenance of social and acceptable behaviour. On the other hand, as with most emotional states, if we push away and defend ourselves from this state we may learn nothing from our mistakes and the shame that arises when we either inadvertently or sometimes deliberately get something wrong or indeed just think we have got something wrong.

Shame begins to emerge for children around about the time they begin to toddle around and get themselves into a spot of inquisitive trouble and have to be told 'no' by Mum, Dad or a close carer. Because children at that age have such a sensitive sense of attachment that they need so very badly, they live with a sense that all minds are the same and that everybody is with them in what they are doing. It is very hard for them when they suddenly realize that a close attachment figure disapproves of them even for a short while. It gives a sense of separation and disconnection that is almost unbearable. This is why, naturally, parents will (hopefully) not be too harsh in their admonishment of a small child who is inevitably going to do the wrong thing. They are a bit like puppies at this age of toddlerhood (about eighteen months) and they genuinely do not know any better. So, softly they are told no and removed from the precipitating danger or the event that they may be heading towards. Time spent being cross with a toddler is time wasted — they simply cannot help themselves yet.

What does shame feel like? It's that red face and that terrible sinking feeling in the stomach that you are alone and cut off and that you got it wrong. It is that sense of 'Oh no, I wish that hadn't happened, that was not right'. In essence, shame is a sense of upset at some miscalculation or mistake that others are going to notice. Of course, as adults in a healthy learning environment we can admit to our errors and 'learn the lessons'. This is highly favourable, but we cannot really avoid the sense of shame — that intrapersonal emotion that tells yourself about yourself, saying, 'Take rapid notice, this will affect your social survival and people will disapprove quickly.' Children are no different: they need to feel the sense that something may have been amiss but they don't need to live in despair for the rest of their lives because of one error. Thus, shame is another of those emotions to be carefully moderated, modulated and mediated (the three Ms) by parents who don't just take this state as something to be bypassed.

Jealousy and envy

Among the complexity of our emotional lives, envy can be most productive if thought about in the right way. Jealousy can transform you into a successful person rather than a jealous person if you allow it to have meaning. Jealousy says, 'I want it too.' When I feel jealous I can be glad that someone has something that I don't have, and I can be aware that somewhere inside I really feel the need to have that too. It could be something superficial and banal like a dress or a pair of shoes, but it is often much more profound than that. Jealousy could encourage you to strive for educational attainment that you perceive someone else to have. Jealousy can be an enriching conversation with ourselves if we take note and reflect on its meaning.

With our children I think it is really important that jealousy becomes a conversation and a narrative on life rather than some mean, hidden little emotion that gets stuffed away in the recesses of our minds, only to jump out and bite us when we least expect it. So if children get jealous over small things like 'He's got this' or 'She's got that', this is such a valuable opportunity not to shame or mock your child but to be with them in their working as a human being.

Jealousy can remind us that we want to be the best we can be and that we feel we might see that best in someone else.

Disgust

I don't need to go into detail in describing how brilliant children can be at expressing their disgust. Smells, in particular, affect their sensory system and evoke this emotion. Disgust is an emotion that primarily keeps us away from something that could potentially harm us, like food that is rotting or human or animal waste that could poison us. Sometimes children need to be told to tone down their reaction a bit if they are in a social situation. I am sure I don't need to go into detail! However, don't be surprised when your kids react with disgust — it means there is something disgusting going on. Be grateful they can be in touch with this emotion that can potentially save their lives or keep them away from bad things, bad people or bad situations.

Surprise and interest

We can have both pleasant and unpleasant surprises. Either way, a surprise is something we did not expect, at a time when we did not expect it, that changes our equilibrium very suddenly, causing an immediate reaction in the sensory system with bristling skin, a sense of freezing, holding of the breath and suspension of logical thought in readiness for either acceptance or reaction. Some children hate surprises, as they feel overwhelmed and upset. Notice how children practise the effect of surprise throughout their lifetime through play. Starting with the game of peekaboo, which is a pleasant surprise, then hide and seek, then jumping out on their parent or carer following hiding, and combine with this the joy they might have in surprising a parent through buying a present. Perhaps a reflection on this childhood rehearsal in preparation for surprise might help us to be aware of how important it is for parents to notice the impact of surprise and whether it is positive or negative.

A parent talks about their journey with emotions

In my childhood family environment, emotions were a matter of shame and something to be hidden. The environment was about control rather than about response. In effect, it was thoroughly dismissive of the emotional lives of children.

Anyone who was upset for too long about anything was referred to as 'a great baby' and sent off to be disgusting in another part of the house. Unsurprisingly, emotions were pushed away and were secretive. Emotion became expressed as part of our dreams and in our behaviour; we were secretly cruel and unkind to each other as we took out our frustrations physically rather than through healthy discussion.

▲▲▲
In conclusion

This has been a journey through emotion which is, in fact, a journey through the map of your inner life and the way it affects thought and feeling. It may feel like a bit of a roller-coaster to you because as you have read these various paragraphs you will have been stimulated and reminded. Perhaps you could give this chapter an emotionally literate response and allow yourself to digest the information before you go on to read more. I had to take a day's break after writing this chapter! I cleaned out my cupboards and reflected with my husband on what makes me upset in life.

You may wonder about the next steps, about how you can make changes in your life and the lives of your children so that they can live more comfortably with their emotions (that is, if they don't already do so). So here is some practical advice for you.

1. Attention to your inner experience should enhance and enrich your life, give you more sense of connectedness to your body and ultimately improved wellbeing. If, however, you find this is not the case and you feel worse about your life then *stop*. Some people are naturally far more logically minded than others and it is wrong to assume everyone is the same or has the same desire to know themselves emotionally. If this is you, then you are not wrong. Even so, stress management, breathing and relaxation are good for everybody. You may get more out of other chapters in this book and you may be a person who is far more suited to cognitive and behavioural approaches (thinking and doing) than to emotional responses. But bear in mind that others have emotional lives, and while this is not a route for you, it may help you to be aware of what is going on inside other people as well as your children, and help you to understand your interactions with them. We are all different and you are not wrong in preferring a different approach.

2. Take plenty of time for rest in your own life, to allow your emotions to find their place and integrate into your thinking. This could mean sitting quietly for twenty minutes in the day, or even twice in the day. Too much activity is often a way to repress or ignore our sensitive responses to life or even stop the thoughts associated with those responses. Stress management and relaxation are a very good, sturdy start to making changes and being more in touch with your body, mind and emotions.

3. Don't frighten or shock your children, partner, friends or relatives by suddenly and drastically changing your responses to emotions. Talk

with them first about your emerging thoughts. You may think that more attention to emotions and inner life is not such a good thing, but you could ask others what they think. Explore this idea.

4. If you feel you have unresolved issues you could go for some counselling sessions to talk things through if you think your friends, partner or family cannot help you. If you are muddled or unresolved on any issues, don't go trying to make changes for others. Wait until you feel secure and understand yourself better. The security you find in yourself will benefit your children and they will love that you are feeling good.

5. A comfortable starting point may be in sharing emotional experiences with your family — maybe watching films, sharing stories and talking about how the people are feeling and what is going on inside them. It's not compulsory to be involved in group hugs or excessive tears. You could all be moved to laughter or even joy, and then you could talk about the meaning behind that joy both for the fictional characters and for yourselves. Talking about fictional others could be a safer place to start.

6. Watch the 2015 Disney film *Inside Out,* the story of a child's life as told by their emotions, from inside their emotional brain. It is a great way to illustrate this chapter.

Symbolic behaviour and managing your child

How many techniques have you heard of for managing behaviour in children? Here are just a few that I have come across. There are techniques for wrapping babies, techniques for putting babies in a highly structured routine, techniques to leave babies on their own, techniques to put them in bed with you, techniques to put children on a naughty step, techniques to mimic the behaviour of small children so as to surprise them, techniques to give children five minutes of quality time a day. I even heard of a technique that teaches newborn babies to regularize their toileting habits.

Most of these techniques cause me some concern because they are about imposing something on children rather than engaging with them and their natural instinct to co-operate, learn from others and thrive and achieve. If you are able to engage this natural sense of co-operation and reciprocal interaction in children from an early age, it is more likely that raising a child from infancy to adulthood will be a joy. It will, however, take time and hard work to achieve this. Here is some matter-of-fact information about managing behaviour in order to elicit co-operation rather than imposing something on your child.

First of all — wherever did we get the idea that telling children off and being hostile to them was useful as a management technique to engage co-operation or even to get children to behave? I have seen many children respond to this style of parenting by becoming even more oppositional and defiant, thus infuriating their already frustrated parents. Hostility, shouting and your cross face are unlikely to help any child learn how to behave. They will just be frightened of you. The first condition to accept in becoming a parent is that your child is going to get things wrong, make mistakes and do things that frustrate and annoy you. It is up to you to learn to manage your frustration and increase your patience while your child is learning about life, rather than to express this exasperation. But there is no harm in being assertive and very firm with your children — this is not the same as being hostile. This brings us to the PATACCAKE formula for thinking about child behaviour, particularly the patience, acceptance and tolerance parts. This is another scenario where your child's behaviour is very much a mirror of *how* you teach them. If you teach them assertively, in a committed way, combined with patience, tolerance and understanding, you are almost guaranteed to raise a child who mirrors and models these behaviours.

Parents often present me with poorly behaved children who they believe are ill or have ADHD or autism, and some children do have these conditions. But this is immaterial. The answer is the same whether the child is on the autistic spectrum/ADHD mix or not — they need to learn how to manage themselves and they will only learn this through you. This is not another parent-blaming opportunity, but it is a very difficult truth that struggling parents often find hard to take on board. In the most extreme cases of behaviour, such as oppositional defiant disorder in young children, it is universally recommended that family therapy is a therapeutic treatment. This is because it is understood clearly that there will be behaviours within the family system and in the parental style that are helping promote the unwanted behaviour. The quicker parents can say, 'Can you show me what it is and how I can change? I understand that I need to learn from this', then the quicker professionals can get on board and support parents in this learning process. It is very difficult indeed when parents blame only their children for their behaviour or choose some mystery condition for their child and don't see that they have to play some part in the cure.

From birth to approximately eighteen months there is very little point in telling your child anything about their behaviour. They will not understand you and their brain is not developed enough to take directions and orders, so they will only do what you are willing to show them to do. Anyone telling off a child of these tender years is making a mistake and simply confusing their child, and sowing the seeds of anxiety. The motor actions of a child this young are entirely due to your containment and management of them and the responses you have to them. If you are tender and thoughtful most of the time with children of this age they will be contented and confident, but caring for them will still be hard work. If you are angry and dismissive, your child will be anxious and discontented and that will be doubly hard work for you. So you have to decide which way you want to play the behaviour card. Do you want to go down the route that creates positive responses in your baby's brain so that they co-operate with you when real behaviour management occurs? Or do you want to close your baby's mind to positive interaction, make them a cross and reactive child who later does not see the point in co-operating with adults and feels confused and disconnected?

For parents of older children my well-worn statement is this: if you are arguing with your child you are getting your strategy wrong. Stop arguing and step back, reflect for some time and then go back to the situation. It is only when you give meaning and learning to life for a child that you make a positive contribution. This does not mean that you have to behave as a model or saintly parent who has no real reactions to life. It simply means that you have to be aware, again, of the impact of your behaviour on your child. If they sense you are angry you will frighten them and they may respond correctly, out of fear. But this will have repercussions later in life — if children really are only responding to bullying and fear they may spend the rest of their lives feeling that if people bully them they have to respond (or indeed, just as bad, it is more likely that they will turn into bullies).

Impact of different parenting styles

In my work with children, adults and families, I have seen a range of parenting styles and the way that these impact children. Neglectful parenting obviously has its consequences; sometimes children are quiet and watchful but more often than not they try to control adults to get a response out of them. Overindulgent parenting results in the same dysfunctional behaviour. I see overindulged children who are monstrous in that they have no social skills, don't respect adults and expect the earth. As a result they are deeply discontent, lacking in any internal or moral connection to themselves, and are often disliked. At both ends of the scale we have unhappy children. Believe it or not, spoilt children are often unhappier because they have such impossible expectations of people and those expectations remain constantly unmet. On the other hand, children who are taught from a sensitive, responsive and well-managed standpoint, where they feel that they are valued as a person, are likely to grow into sensitive and responsive adults. But this is challenging, so let's look at some of the challenges throughout the parenting spectrum.

Emotional connection is key

My proposition to you is that behaviour management is secondary to the emotional connection that you create with your child. How you manage their behaviour depends on their stage of development. These aspects form a triangle: the child, their stage of development and the emotional state of the relationship. Therefore, the overall outcome of a child's behaviour depends on more than just what a child can and cannot do. If behaviour depended on these things alone (i.e. what they can do when you tell them) then we would have a very rigid form of parenting. On the other hand, we cannot depend on the quality of the emotional relationship alone. This may form a style of over-permissive, over-involved parenting whereby the child is excessively hooked into the parent emotionally and has no sense of themselves and their own needs. This can breed anxious, highly dependent and guilty children, and this style of parenting leads to as many problems as the rigid style of parenting. A mindful balance that bears in mind all of these aspects is likely to be a synthesis of what children really need — feeding their sensitivity, their need for structure and their emotional security combined with realistic expectations and appropriate communication.

A behavioural approach

It may help you to understand something about techniques that are only based on behaviour therapy (i.e. that attend to a child's actions). Most behaviour modification techniques are based on the work of B.F. Skinner, whose work and thinking was based on the famously known work of Ivan Pavlov with his dogs in the 1900s.[1,2] You may recall that his dogs produced saliva ready to eat, even when meat was not present for their meal, because Pavlov had trained them to respond to a conditioned stimulus, which was his tuning fork. The dogs were making an association with the sound of the tuning fork because their master had taught them to do so. B.F. Skinner's work is based on the idea of positive reinforcement — that is, when a certain behaviour is given a positive response, that behaviour will increase and when it is given a negative response it will decrease.[3] The most common form of negative reinforcement from parents is when they take something, for example a computer game, from the child if they are misbehaving and then it is given back after a certain period of time. There is nothing wrong with this idea and it will work perfectly well, but there are also some limitations to this style of responding to children.

The main limitation of responding in a behavioural-only manner is that you will only achieve temporary gains. It is likely that your child will become very familiar with having their electronic equipment removed and that they will need something else to stimulate their behaviour system in due course. Also, parents do need to explore the thoughts and feelings of their child when taking this approach. If you take away your child's electronic equipment because he or she is mean to their little brother, it might stop them being mean for a while. But you still haven't explored your child's thoughts and feelings about the pesky little brother and you have missed an opportunity to develop your relationship with them. All you have done is exerted your power over your child with your behavioural response. Ultimately, children are born to question power and as they get older they will challenge power and want more from you, so behavioural techniques may work for a while but they won't hold true for ever.

The shortfall with the very popular naughty step is that it might well work for small children but you are not going to be putting your fifteen-year-old on any naughty step for very long. It is far better to encourage a child, particularly a toddler or preschooler, to sit quietly with you while they calm their behaviour down and then talk with them about it, giving them your expertise as an adult and showing them how to regulate their behaviour through calm responses, emotional support and good talking and understanding. This will shape your child's behaviour, shaping their brain towards co-operation and kindness rather than anger and rage. In my view, to isolate any child is a very limited response indeed and often adults need a much broader and compassionate view of child behaviour.

The best position with regard to behaviour management is to have plenty of behavioural cash in the bank, so to speak. As a mind-minded parent, think about the long game and this will already prepare you for dealing with your child's behaviour. Thus, if you are constantly reinforcing good behaviour through the 'cash' payment of praise and attention to your child, you are putting plenty of profit into their behavioural bank (i.e. their brain). Your child will gain a strong sense that it is rewarding to co-operate because this will be reinforced on an almost daily basis by the things that you say to them, the narrative that can be part of their daily life. So when times do arise where there is a rupture in that smooth flow of communication between you, your child will want to heal that rupture just as much as you do, and they only need you to show them how to do this. Mind-minded and Mind Kind parents know that it is inevitable that children will be awkward at times and that their needs may clash with yours, or that they will want more than they can actually have. They will see this as an opportunity for their child to learn and grow rather than a disappointing time of argument and failure with winners and losers.

Children are often selfish and inconsiderate in their behaviour because they are still in the process of becoming civilized. At these times they need to be shown and given the right information about how to act appropriately. Do not reward selfish behaviour. This kind of response is known in behavioural terms as 'selective ignoring' (i.e. not giving any positive attention or reward to undesirable behaviours). Children need to learn to be in command of their primitive behaviours and find healthy solutions, and for this they will take their cues from you. This is a learning process which is very different from children being made to feel shame for bad behvaviour.

Some of the following information might help you to sink into your role as a Mind Kind parent utilizing the PATACCAKE skills of patience, acceptance, tolerance, attunement, commitment, compassion, awareness, kindness and empathy.

Babies

Babies need your attention and sensitivity at all times. If they receive this they will start to adapt and socialize, and rely on and enjoy relationships with people as a source of support (depending on their temperament and genetic predisposition). They will naturally want to co-operate. Sensitivity as a human response comes to babies quite naturally. We respond to their vulnerability, but our own sensitivity may be blocked if we were dealt with in an insensitive manner as a baby. You might not feel it is right to respond to a baby as quickly as possible; you may have values inside that say 'Leave her to cry' or 'She is only crying'. However, what these attitudes bring to your baby is a sense of despair, and this is why I simply cannot recommend any parenting programs that advocate leaving a baby alone for long lengths of time (unless, of course, they are sleeping naturally and clearly need space to themselves).

Babies are blameless

A key developmental fact about your baby's behaviour from birth to toddlerhood is that *your baby is never ever naughty*. It is simply not possible for a baby to be naughty. (More specifically, I would say that any child under the age of seven cannot be considered to be just plain naughty.) Babies and toddlers can only be considered as not having enough of your attention or enough management from you, enough guidelines, enough of the right information or enough thoughtfulness. They might feel unsafe or discontent, or they might forget the rules for a while, but babies do not intentionally go about being naughty — they do not have the capability. Your baby can only show you that they need something like comfort, warmth, food, affection or play, and sometimes babies just feel plain awkward about life and have moments of frustration and feeling fed up. They get bored and need stimulation or they just don't feel right, and even though that may appear fussy, it is not their fault. They can only rely on you to put things right for them and they cannot help those fussy moments and cannot put it right for themselves.

Some days you might feel overwhelmed by your baby's needs. Whether you are a mother or father, adoptive parent or carer it matters not — because you are human you will have days when you are feeling down, struggling with something or feeling under the weather. Sadly, your baby does not particularly register these reasons and cease their demands on you, demands which will seem relentless when you are not coping. Often at these times, babies can even be more fractious, more needy and they may even be affected by your state and start to react to that. Find people who can support you at these times while you take a break to settle your mind — this will be both in your best interests and the best interests of your baby. It is, without question, very hard but you have to find a way through; opting out is not a choice. If the worst comes to the worst, rather than taking out any negative emotions on your baby, put them down in a safe place and leave them for five minutes while you recover your senses. Five minutes of breathing space and a sip of tea might make the difference.

Babies are born to pass on their demands to you and in doing so they are only doing what is instinctive to them. It is up to you to regulate them as best you can and with as much of a positive state as you can. I would be concerned about any parent who does not find their baby demanding at times because it might mean they are not noticing their baby's needs.

The ultimate key to managing a baby is your ability to attune (tune in and sense) to the baby's communications. If you can remember the 'attunement rule' you can perhaps stand back and reset your own behavioural stance and attitude to your baby.

Toddlers

When your baby grows into a toddler, you will realize that having an infant was so simple and hardly took up any of your time! Toddlers are busy people on a mission to explore the world and you have to keep up. As with babies, *a toddler cannot be naughty.* They certainly cannot formulate malintent or make a plan to wind a parent up. I hear so many parents say 'He is just winding me up', but this is not possible. A child may become excited and exuberant and they may lack boundaries. Or they may be disturbed and troubled, and hard to settle. There is only one person who is going to make a difference to that behaviour and that is you.

It is important to understand a toddler mentally and emotionally as well as to manage their environment. They are prone to explore and have little control over their motor actions, so they will see an object and head immediately for it if it interests them. This is their instinct to be alive at work, and it can be seen from a perspective of absolute joy and fascination if you are able to hold this in mind. But on a bad day it might be seen as a tiring nuisance when your child becomes annoying. Toddlers are not doing anything other than getting on with the business of being a toddler. This means they are often moving around with exuberance, feeling pleased about exploring, not really knowing what is dangerous and what is not. It means loving your attention, loving comfort from you and needing a very good routine and a very safe environment. It means being with you as well as playing with you and it means that a lot of adult time and attention is needed in order to regularize and manage them.

The use of a playpen is fine if it gives you a much-needed short break from your toddler. They were developed for a reason and are not 'mini prisons giving the child the impression of living behind bars' as I heard one beautifully liberal parent exclaim. Playpens provide an opportunity for a moment of respite for *you* so that you can regain your equilibrium, re-establish your position and galvanize your resources while your busy toddler is in a safe place. Equilibrium is an essential tool as a parent managing behaviour, and you need to be in the right frame of mind to do this. It's much healthier to pop a toddler into a playpen for half an hour with some soft toys where they can see Mum or Dad or their carer, than to have an exasperated carer or parent who is going to scream at them in frustration. They will become used to this as a familiar place of respite for them — a healthy rest from all that exploring. From all that you have read so far, which parental choice of behaviour do you think is going to set you up for the future and give you the better outcome?

Toddlerhood only lasts for about a year and a half before your child heads into the mind of a preschooler. You can decide to enjoy this busy time of learning or you can let it exasperate and frustrate you. If you spend money on anything at this stage of a child's life let it be on cushions and soft play items so that your toddler can climb and toddle as much as they like. It's also a great idea to find friends who also have children, who can take over for half an hour and perhaps watch two toddlers while you take a break and then swap over. Don't do things with a child that will cause frustration to you — be Mind Kind to yourself and your child. For example, don't take them shopping if you can avoid it. If you are really stuck for childcare and must take your toddler shopping with you, take their brain needs into consideration. They will either be terribly bored and frustrated by being strapped into their stroller or they will be overstimulated by too much colour, noise and excitement. Make some choices to help regulate your child's responses and behaviour. You could give yourself more time and pace yourself, recognizing that it will be a bewildering and frustrating experience for your toddler unless you are watching them and managing their situation.

If you are smart in parenting little people it can be such a joy to watch their learning, which vastly accelerates as their brain develops. They might be sleeping through the night by this stage so you can keep them in a sturdy routine, which will increase their happiness and security. Get them into bed early after a bath and feed and get some space to yourself. This is the kind of management that you need so that you can survive. If necessary, settle toddlers by sitting quietly with them for some time. This will both comfort them and get them used to the idea that you will leave the bedroom and that everything should be quiet. Make sure everything is soothing, familiar and routine around bedtime. Children feel much more secure when they are in a routine and Mind Kind parents should take this into consideration to make life comfortable for both themselves and their child. Aim for a blissful time of regulation and make regular corrections to your routine so that you maximize every opportunity. You don't have to get everything right first time around.

Toddler to preschooler

By this age (two and a half to three years old) children are chattering all the time about their experiences. They are inquiring and inquisitive. This is a pivotal stage of development when little people start to notice something very startling about life — that other people have minds as well as their own sense of their own mind. This can be a problem for them because it clashes with their egocentricity, or the idea that 'I am the only show in town'. I have heard this referred to in modern-day parenting terms as 'little king' or 'little emperor' syndrome, which can be rather misleading. I will go over this stage of development in more detail in the chapters on child development, where you will begin to understand why your toddler starts to have tantrums about the difficulty of asserting their own will compared with the will of others.

Children of this age need a lot of information about what and why things are as they are. Behaviourally, they may still not understand why they cannot have Dad's screwdriver to run around with and this can cause them great frustration. If you understand that this — how to deal with others — is the key lesson at this stage of their life, you can be more patient, kind and tolerant of your preschooler; you can be more Mind Kind, more mind minded and less Mind Blind. In understanding these things you'll also use the kindness and tolerance of PATACCAKE, because children need patience and positive responses (rather than reactivity) in order to learn.

Since every stage of development marks the springboard to the next stage of development, you can start to see why the preschool period of life is so precious in laying down experiences that say to a child, 'We are with you in this exciting world that is full of learning every day.' Children continue their journey towards security, but more importantly they learn that when they get things wrong people help them to learn rather than get frustrated and full of rage with them. Because they are treated with kindness and calmness they will internalize these experiences and they will, in turn, become kind and calm. They will learn to manage their own frustration in a positive way. They will observe how you regulate yourself around them and they will follow your lead and regulate their own difficult emotions.

Middle childhood years

There is no reason for children of this age to be a nuisance in terms of their behaviour but there are, of course, many challenges for parents during this time. These are heavenly years of childhood when children are enjoying their increased independence, as well as enjoying a connection to their family. This is when children between the ages of seven and fourteen are making friendship groups and learning about socializing. School becomes very important both for learning and as a venue for friendships and connections with others.

It is definitely not too late for children to learn the fundamentals of behaviour in their middle childhood years if they have not grasped them (or social skills) yet. If you start to notice your child does not understand some of the rules and does not fit in with their peer group, or is struggling with belonging, try to uncover the reasons why. Fundamentally, the first step is to observe what is going on so that you can begin to understand how your child is feeling. There can be many factors that contribute to difficulties when children feel that they are different — it is not necessarily down to parenting.

Children of this age form strong peer groups and networks and they can start to get a little bossy about who can and cannot belong to their group. They like group norms and can be quite conservative and conformist. They are at a stage in life when morality starts to emerge and are also quite fixed about mixing with members of the opposite sex. Freud described this stage of development as the stage of latency (between the ages of seven and eleven). In evolutionary terms, this is for a good reason — we simply don't want children of this age engaging in sexual activity as it is not good for them. There will be minor flirtations and curiosity about members of the opposite sex but on the whole there is an inherent message to keep some distance.

Behaviour management for children of this age requires logical responses and good explanations, and you need to provide clear, strong routines and structures. Children must learn to adhere to rules, and the boundaries are not to be knocked down too easily unless there is room for reasonable negotiation and a good conversation about right and wrong and making good choices. If you are clear and solid about rules it will help your child to feel secure, just as babies feel secure when they feel a routine around them. It means that we ask children to adhere to rules and accept that some of the time they will forget about them and genuinely need reminding, more than once. They will also test boundaries and we need to accept that this is part of their personality development and brain development. We all test boundaries as part of our learning and we need to give children a shame-free chance to put their mistakes right.

At this age, children are mentally and emotionally beginning to invest in relationships outside of the home and especially at school, and this needs to be taken seriously. We need not be surprised, then, that this, along with their social survival, matters a great deal to them. We need to listen to their stories about who did this and that and the mistakes that they and other children are making in making and breaking friends. We need to take time to be interested in the stories that begin to emerge. In doing this, we begin to build a platform that shows we are interested in our child's life and their thoughts about their own relationships (i.e. the way they start to think about people and the ways they act). We are creating a buffer for them around the stresses and strains of life outside the home, but most of all we are developing our own role as a resource for a child as they prepare to move into their next stage of development — those teenage years where, quite frankly, you will become totally dispensable as a parent on some days and totally needed and wanted on others.

If you consider that the seven glorious years of middle childhood are about joining groups, learning to develop individual friendships and managing the rules of a minor society while playing and having fun, you will make a good start to understanding the teen years, which are yet a further extension of this journey into society.

Teen years

These, too, can be wonderful years for parenting rather than an opportunity for your home to be turned into a war zone full of aggression and frayed tempers. Once again, management of children aged thirteen to eighteen relies on a good balance between recognizing their developmental tendencies and needs, and a sense of control and management that provides security and recognition of their thoughts and feelings. Young people of this age have shifting sands under their feet. One day they are conquering the world and feeling very powerful and grown up, the next they revert to five-year-old tactics and need parental support, guidance, love and nurturing. You have to learn to roll with the punches and take some rejection to a reasonable degree (note, though, that I do not mean physical aggression, which is not tolerable as a form of communication either from parent to child or child to parent). I am describing here the ability to tolerate the rejection that teenagers will inevitably show to their parents. This is generally to enhance their growing sense of autonomy and independence, which naturally happens as their brain continues to develop. Quite simply, they cannot help being awkward and at times rejecting. Gone is the idealization of the parent, as can happen in middle childhood, and boom — you have a dismissive young person who thinks that most things about you are at best worthy of laughter and at worst worthy of rejection. Either way, the poor things are dictated by their hormones and neurochemistry to begin to push away the very people on whom they have depended all their lives.

Some parents find this intolerable and retaliate with either a sense of rage or upset. Retaliation is not a mind-minded response. What is needed is a sensible understanding that, to achieve autonomy and adulthood, your teenager has to have some sense of putting you aside. They might find many creative ways to do this. One of the main routes is to dismiss, avoid and diminish your 'stupid' rules and regulations. So your smooth-running household becomes chaotic and you have something new to learn about your 'control issues'. This is not to say that behaviour management is not possible with teenagers. There are many things you still have to manage and help your child to think about: staying out late, not knowing where they are, drug taking, alcohol use, sex before the legal age of consent, self-harm as a self-regulation technique, to name but a few of the things that are going to run out of control if you don't have some management. In order to achieve this when your kids are almost adults, you need to keep your head in ways you will never before have thought possible. You have to acknowledge that your child is throwing off the dreadful shackles of your parenting, that they are flexing their muscles and that they want to feel free. On the other hand, they need you quite a lot — they are not totally independent and are probably still living under your roof, and you require some respect.

The balance between a rigid and an excessively liberal approach is the pathway best known to help parents at this stage. Find a balance between being an authoritarian, military-style parent from a totalitarian state and an excessively lax former hippy parent who likes to hang out and get down with the kids. A Mind Kind response is tolerant and understanding while teaching children that they have to continue to respect others even if they do not like them very much. This is a parent with dignity and authority in their communications.

In their exploration of their world, teenagers need both encouragement and protection, freedom as well as limits. It is in developing an approach that is tolerant and communicative that we might be able to inoculate our teenagers against stress, anxiety, depression and self-harm.

Notes from a parent trying to understand behaviour management

When I reflected on this [their own childhood] I realized it was because there was not a lot of room for negotiation on my behaviour and that I was subject to rigid and unforgiving parenting. So, the good news is that I know exactly how this feels. The bad news is that it is not very nice and never gains good results. You may have a kid who does everything you want but you don't have a child who feels loved, cherished and happy in themselves and who can talk about their thoughts and feelings.

Rigid and unforgiving parenting may get you a result in the first place, but it will not gain you a secure and happy child. It may gain you a resentful and withdrawn child who feels hurt at a sense of rejection and lack of control over his or her life. I know that is how I felt most of the time. Children usually turn this resentment in on themselves and it leads to low self-esteem, self-doubt and lack of confidence at best. At worst a child can become utterly avoidant of relationships because they no longer have any faith in their ability to relate as they have no power whatsoever and are afraid of being hurt.

On the other side of that rigid parenting approach was a lack of control and management over issues that mattered, such as the way my brothers and sisters were interacting or fighting with each other. The results of this were catastrophic in my life, leading to anxiety and stress in my adult years.

▲▲▲
In conclusion

Parents today are under such pressure in every direction, starting from financing a home for children in which they can feel warm and safe. In many families, both parents work, meaning that time is always short. For parents and carers who stay at home, they might have enough time on their hands to manage but then find that money is possibly short and they spend long hours parenting while the other parent is out making money. Those at home can lose out on career development and have another set of anxieties to deal with.

With the basic issue of a roof over the family's head organized, it all boils down to the ability to budget, living within your means while managing the relentless tsunami of wants, shoulds and oughts that head your way. You have to buy this, you have to have that, etc. You don't have to have any material things to be a fantastically lovable parent, one who can manage their child's behaviour so that they grow up to manage themselves. It is, however, a strain on modern families. The demands are relentless and without doubt children need time and attention given to behaviour management. It is hard to focus on children's thoughts and feelings when all you need done is the task at hand. This really concerns me more than anything about parenting today, that parents are run into the ground with worry and stress before they even get to think about parenting issues. So to ask you to take time to reflect — I hardly dare do that. But if you can make a plan that builds in downtime for you and all your family, and if you can bear in mind that behaviour is only part of what you see about a child — only a symptom or an outcome of what is going on for them — you will be able to be more Mind Kind and it is likely that your child will have a felt sense that you understand them. In my view this is the real meaning of behaviour. Behaviour is a symbol of what goes on inside the child.

Adversity

Helping children through
difficult times

It is a given that none of us is immune from the apparently uncontrollable ups and downs of life. We are all affected by change, some of it might be pleasant and some will challenge and threaten us. It is also a given that being human includes being able to manage ourselves during adversity so that we can achieve the best possible outcome, but we need to learn the skills to manage and face this change. Mind Kind and more realistic parenting equips and prepares you to help your children at times of stress.

Many parents get anxious and worried and need reassurance on the best way to support and help their children through difficult times. We have already established that parental stress deeply affects children. You could be experiencing an extreme event such as the loss or illness of a family member, bankruptcy, poverty or even flood, war or murder; it could also be an expected life event such as exams at school, moving house or changing class, or an organic event such as puberty or a new baby in the family. Whatever the event or issue, the instinct to support and protect needs to remain in place as much as parentally possible, and if it is not possible then this task should be taken over by someone who is in a position to support and protect. For a child, a crisis is a crisis and an upset is an upset, whether it's a struggle with being last in maths or a dreadful life event. It all needs our attention.

Below are some suggested responses and behaviours to bring you closer to finding solutions to support your child during periods of adversity. These suggestions could just as easily apply to yourself at times of stress in your own life.

Show your child you want to give attention

Things can go wrong at times of crisis if parents lose their own footing and begin to slide into their own anxiety and despair about any given situation. They forget that their thoughts and self-management are going to be part of the solution. You are only human and you may be trying to cope with something that is difficult for you too. While it is healthy to be realistic with children, we don't want them to have to watch our decline into hopelessness and despair. This puts responsibility for managing back onto them and that is a heavy burden for a young mind. So you need to self-evaluate. If you think you are not coping with any given situation in a way that gives your child confidence, then be smart and enlist the help of someone you can trust with the mind of your child and also someone who is going to be kind, loving, thoughtful and respectful to you both in this situation.

Hopefully, friends and family will support you, but we don't all have loving and supportive families of our own or they may not be near, in which case professional services may be able to offer better help. Unfortunately, if you don't have your own loving, supportive or even mindful family you could be vulnerable to support from the wrong people who are not trustworthy. In this situation you need to be even more effective in searching for services and it is best to start with seeking information from your doctor, schools, registered charities or professional bodies who have some duty of care towards you. The major point here is that your confidence in any given situation will be almost equal in quality and style to the confidence that your child will have in any given situation — remembering that children are such strong mirrors of our own inner states. So if you don't feel confident of your own ability you can search for the best possible next best thing, which may turn out to be ideal.

You could also read and search for websites that give good information. For example, many parents find websites such as Mumsnet.com useful for support, reading and advice. I have managed to send plenty of individuals to charities for free life crisis counselling and therapy when they cannot pay for private work and do not wish to wait for state psychological services.

Establish a conversation with your child

It is very easy during stressful events to find yourself lost for words. People are often of the mindset that to 'provoke' a conversation will be harmful rather than making things better. For example, when a child has lost a parent, I have frequently heard well-meaning parents and family friends say he is 'best left so that he forgets all about it'. Children don't forget a lot of things they experience in their lives and many therapy rooms demonstrate this point, with adults wishing to discuss and resolve the things that others thought they were forgetting when they were children! There are certainly times when it might be helpful to support children to decrease the amount of time they spend worrying about a given event if they are becoming overly anxious, obsessive or depressed about it, thus encouraging them to be in control of the problem and their thinking, rather than the problem being in control of them. But even this kind of scenario requires that first a dialogue about the problem be established.

It does not matter if you have not previously been skilled at establishing dialogue or conversation in your child's life. You may have been very good at other things like playing, supporting and having fun, which means you have been establishing a parental relationship on which it is perfectly possible to now start building a conversational bridge. On the other hand, if your parenting has been intrusive and you have tried to get too much conversation out of your child, you may need to learn the value of quiet support that is subtler, leaving children to be the masters of their conversation with you and using their own minds.

On the whole, many years of supporting parents tells me that it is better to raise an issue with a child from the right stance, rather than hope it will go away. One parent who was sure his daughter was coping with the death of her mother (because she never said a word) now has an adult daughter who won't speak with him because he never raised the issue and did not appear to be bothered. Any attempt at conversation about difficult things does not have to be a one-off event, as children may well wish to hide secret feelings from you — and every child has a right to their secret thoughts and feelings. You do not have to know them all. You may have to be quite subtle, perhaps talking about another child who had a similar problem or about a problem you had in childhood as an example. Be considered and use a positive curious stance — 'I am worried sick about you so you'd better come out with it' is never going to be encouraging. Setting the ground for good conversations and simple heart-to-heart honesty will always be helpful. It is more important to think about creating this as part of your home environment than it is forcing any conversations to happen.

Here are some possible opening lines for you:

» 'Some children find it hard when ...'

» 'I remember that Aunty/Uncle used to struggle with that and then we found her some help ...'

» 'We are all good at some things and struggle with others. I used to struggle with ...'

» 'We all need help at times — I remember I used to need help with ...'

» 'You are so good at ... but I wonder if you might struggle with ...'

» 'I hope I can help you with that, I always love to help you. My brain is at the ready to think it through.'

» 'No, it's fine you don't want to talk right now. Here's a hug anyway. I know you'll let me know if you wish.'

Often our expectations can be too high in terms of the sort of responses and results that we get when starting a conversation with our child. Don't expect to achieve your goal first time around. This is not a target-focused exercise. This is not going to be the sort of conversation you get in the office where you cut a deal in as few words as possible. Don't expect an elegant and coherent response. You might get pushed away, you might get a denial, your child might ignore you and they might be cross. Any response should be welcome and the type of response gives you more information about what your child is thinking and what to do next time around. It is your job only to encourage and accept. We want to give children a sense of control over their problem, rather than a sense that you are going to get to the root of the problem in one conversation and solve it. Most problems require sustained attention to be resolved.

Your response is important

Your response to your child's response is even more important than the way in which you initially raise the issue. A PATACCAKE response that includes words that are kind, calm, accepting and understanding is where you need to be. This could be expressed through humour or simply through kind words. You might need to practise by talking with a friend or partner first. These conversations are a work in progress rather than a completed object; you are building the platform to connection and understanding.

Kind words are free and cost you nothing and they always impact a child's heart and wellbeing. Even if a child never speaks with you, they will remember your kindness. I highly recommend an excellent and classic book for helping parents to speak with their children called *How to Talk so Kids will Listen and Listen so Kids will Talk*.[1] This book must have changed the lives of thousands of parents and their relationships with their children, just through teaching a very simple method of encouraging communication, most of all by helping parents to listen.

Your emotional attitude towards your child will set up a positive environment for communication. Lots of practice with words will come next.

Take responsibility rather than taking the blame

Guilty parents are easy to come by. A parent who feels guilty has the potential to be a sensitive parent, but they do have to be careful that their guilt does not engulf them in shame and turn them into a weak, ineffective parent with no authority. All parents make parenting errors and it is always hard to own up to the fact that you may have failed or upset your child. It is far better to accept what you might have got wrong and then advance your thinking by recalling the things you did and do get right. Reassure yourself that all parents are prone to lapses, inattention and not being there at the right time. That can all be put right with a small amount of self-reflection and self-honesty. Such honesty leads to more mindfulness as a parent rather than less effectiveness. You don't have to ask your child for forgiveness as much as you have to acknowledge yourself and your vulnerabilities that led to what went wrong. If you cannot be compassionate to yourself about your failings, you are less likely to show your child a realistic compassion, or you may even show them a false compassion and they will always be unsure because their felt sense will tell them that you are not authentic. Children are brilliant detectives on authenticity and the felt sense of experience.

Plan

A flexible and adaptive plan for support is a roadmap to change and a more happy and beneficent future for your child. A rigidly built plan that is not open to adaptation is simply a tool to beat yourself up with, to make you feel bad and to make your child feel awful too. The beauty of a parent constructing a plan for support and change is that it can be sensitive to your child's needs and uniqueness and it can be something you can build together. It is always better to work at change together, as children will be sensitive if there is a change in your agenda towards them.

The rules of change management are that you should help people to have some control over the change in order to decrease anxiety as much as possible. So, whether you are making a plan to help a child reduce weight and get fitter or you are making a plan to support a child with the unique circumstances of bereavement, it is still a plan for change and psychological development for you both. You can make it a joy and a journey, or you can make it an act of despair and a punishment (I will leave it to you to decide which is going to work best).

Sample plans

This is a list of suggested plans that could be built with a child to help raise their self-esteem and confidence.

- » 'We will go for a walk every day to help you feel full of energy and strong.'

- » 'Mum and Dad will check in every day to see how you are feeling and check on any worries. We will measure your feelings on a scale of 0 to 10.'

- » 'We will choose a new activity that you really enjoy and want to do and that you can learn to be good at.'

» 'Dad will take time out in the evening to help you with homework.'

» 'You can invite a new friend over for a play date and tea once a week.'

» 'Mum will tell your teacher you need help with confidence building if you wish.'

» 'We will get you to bed a little earlier so you'll get good sleep.'

» 'We'll all eat fresh vegetables every day and give you yoghurt so you'll get good bacteria in your stomach. You can have fruit in your lunch box and Mum will make sure you cut back on sugary snacks that make you feel bad in the end.'

» 'We will look at our plan every week and see what you want to change or add and we will see what has gone well.'

Note that this plan costs nothing but your time, energy and commitment.

Monitor

Success is achieved more often through a specific plan for change and with the support of those around you in your environment. Thus, as an adult planning to give up smoking it is more likely you'll achieve your goal if your friends support you rather than encourage you towards just one more smoke with them. Combined with that support from those around you, you might plan to use the support of substitute cigarettes at your most vulnerable times of the day for a cigarette, like break times. So a clear plan, shared with supportive people, is going to be most effective.

The best plans are monitored for necessary adaptation and change. For example, if you are engaged in the very sensitive task of helping a child to slim down and you notice the time of day they are most hungry, provide either a meal at that hungry time of the day or plenty of the healthy snacks such as fruit and vegetable sticks. If your child says they are not hungry for breakfast you might save up their quality snack for break time when they are starving, so that they don't fill themselves with chips and sweets. This way a child's organic self is taken into consideration and we know that the evolutionary and organic aspect of the mind likes to be considered when change is happening.

Equally, if you are supporting a child through depression you will benefit enormously from a plan that includes positive experiences that achieve the greatest degree of joy. So if rollerblading makes your depressed junior scared — and if he or she cannot overcome that — then stop it and factor in something else on a more frequent basis. On the other hand, if they love the excitement then keep them doing it.

Keep monitoring the progress of your plan. Notice the detail and work with it, then you are dancing with your child and dancing can only make us happy.

Simple changes to enhance wellbeing and mental health

There is a range of general behaviours and activities that can enhance mental health and wellbeing in children, as well as adults, and it is important not to underestimate the impact that small changes can have on the minds and lives of children and families. Small changes can make a big difference to reorganizing a life and allowing a brain to flow more freely. They do not have to cost money at all and can create a sense of harmony and wellbeing for families.

A definition of good mental health would be that the energy in the brain is flowing evenly and getting on with the task of survival and engagement with society. What is it that makes the energy in our brain more even, well-balanced, harmonious and free-flowing? The brain is fed by the senses and therefore any activity that acknowledges the important roles of the senses will optimize the relationship between mind and body. So smell, touch, sound, sight and taste are your target. For centuries, sages, mystics and religious institutions have understood the impact of smell on the brain, using incense as a way of enhancing a state of mind.

Here are some examples of helping a child's sensory system, to help them stabilize and experience wellbeing and increased contentment.

Smell

If you have stressed children you could help them by burning essential oils while they are watching television and then taking note of the impact. This small act has had remarkable results in my clinic where children sniff the air and collapse into the chair enjoying the smell in the room. Parents do this too.

Children in sessions with me enjoy choosing their own special smell from a simple and inexpensive range — peppermint, orange, lavender and lemon tangerine with vanilla are top favourites. Without any effort at all, just by using the olfactory system and showing interest, parents can quietly show that they are interested their child's wellbeing. It also gives children a smell to remember and associate with relaxation. I will often take note of a child's specific and favourite oil and will have it in the room when they arrive. I am always confident that children who smell their favourite smell will soon feel a sense of relaxation and this then helps them to talk about what is under the surface of their everyday mind. I also do this for adults. This smell will forge strong associations in a child's mind for the future and it is especially nice if a special smell can remind them of home with emotion. Just as we react strongly to bad smell, we also react just as immediately to a good smell. It is clear that pleasant smells create wellbeing and engage the limbic system in a soothing reaction; then we are already making progress and creating happy memories.

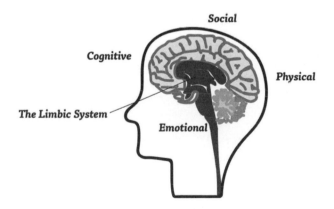

I know that aromatherapy may have 'hippy' type associations but if you look on the shelves of any leading pharmacy these days you will find an array of aromas. It is possible that we still haven't tapped into the full impact of aromatherapy for wellbeing and that this form of stress management will become even more favourable in the future in medical settings.

Touch

Utilizing touch can be achieved in many simple, effective ways to enhance relaxation and a shift in a child's state of mind. Parents can give a hand massage, foot massage or head massage to their children if they like this form of touch. Some children do not like this and see this form of touch as unusual or intrusive, which must be respected. Every child has the right to dictate the experiences of their body and children should understand 'safe' touch and touch that they do not want. (I am referring to a child–parent/ carer relationship. Clearly, professionals are not going to be engaged in touch with children except in medical or extenuating circumstances.) A fed-up child who has had a hard day at school may rethink their problems or even share them with a parent and find resolution if their anxiety is reduced by a relaxing hand massage. This is such a simple and enjoyable (and free) way to relate to our children and to each other.

If children are really anxious, there are many skilled and highly trained massage therapists who will give massage and you can be present for this. Children can keep their clothes on to help them feel safe. I worked with one childcare charity who provided massage for stressed children and this was one of their most popular support services, with the massage therapist rushed off her feet and parents learning in the sessions how to help their child's stress through massage. It just proved how much children need physical reassurance.

If you are not such a touchy-feely parent there are plenty of foot massagers around and there is even a wire head massager that I have seen children enjoying playing with. If they learn properly from parents about positive touch, it can be part of their emergency first aid kit for life.

Movement

This can include yoga, Pilates, dance, stretching, walking, running or anything that gets you co-ordinating mind and body like cycling, skating, skipping or scooting. These things do not have to cost money and you don't have to go to classes, although this can be fun. Current research suggests that you only have to do half an hour a day of moderate exercise such as walking or dancing to be in good condition. It is fun to do yoga with children on the lounge floor for twenty minutes and you could incorporate breathing and balancing exercises to balance the mind.

There are many books around on relaxation movement with children, and I would recommend *Ladybird's Remarkable Relaxation*.[2] This kind of habit could set your children up for life in taking responsibility for their wellbeing behaviours and you can share moments with them through a simple walk or jog together. My family still has great fun in remembering the time we went out and played golf together — unfortunately they were laughing at me but it's still a happy memory for us all.

Mindfulness practice

Any form of quietness is great downtime for kids, whose minds can become overactive. Mindfulness practice can take many forms — it is simply about finding ways to keep your mind still. I encourage children in my sessions to use an egg timer. They focus on the sand falling through the timer and cannot wait for it to finish, but of course during this time their mind is still and focused and I have got them to meditate.

Mindfulness can involve encouraging a child to look at a beautiful picture, which you can do with them, and see the lovely things that you can see. Or you could focus your mind on a view. More traditional methods involve sitting quietly and focusing on your breathing. Children will take to this if they are encouraged and I have seen children transform their attitude and anxiety in seconds when they are taught to sit quietly and allow the mind to settle. In these practices children are increasing the flexibility, and therefore the ability, of their own mind. The key skill is to focus more on less, and give your mind a chance to relax. There are many mental illnesses, such as anxiety and depression, which can be effectively treated when people are able to be aware of how they overuse their mind and how much more they need to relax. This is the same for children.

A beautiful object such as a stone or shell could be something lovely on which a child can focus. There are also a lot of 'mindfulness' colouring books available that are designed especially to help the mind focus on one thing only and therefore to relax and stop worrying.

Monitoring moods

Moodscope.com offers a great opportunity to monitor your own moods and ups and downs. It is a brilliant tool for parents who are suffering from anxiety and depression, despair and even manic or compulsive tendencies. Once you have checked on your own moods then check your children's moods and help them keep a daily graph of their moods (you would have to do theirs with them at first). You can keep a graph over the years as to how your moods develop. It is highly likely that if you monitor your moods they will improve and this will improve general mood-literacy and understanding in your household, opening up conversations about how you all are. Also have a look at moodjuice.scot.nhs.uk, a great interactive website to help children work with and understand their moods.

Food

Food and mood are an equation not to be missed. Mood food is not a myth — there are foods that will enhance mood and even help people with depression. These are foods high in healthy oils such as lean chicken, avocado, salmon, brazil nuts and almonds. They are very simple to prepare and could even be special treats for children. Salmon is not expensive if it is bought fresh, and if you are on a budget you can always buy the fresh salmon that is just about to go out of date and cook it on the same day, serving it with a green salad drizzled in olive oil. You can monitor the situation and see which foods seem to provide a lift for your children. You could also share the baking of bread with your children, which is incredibly cheap and so very easy. Simply grab a basic bread recipe from the internet and encourage children to help you bake delicious, healthy bread that they can enjoy sharing. There is nothing simpler to do together, nor more mood enhancing. The website for the UK-based mental health charity Mind has great information on the link between mind and food (mind.org.uk).

Oils that are high in omega-3 fatty acids are protective of the nervous system. Alternatively you could give your child some oil through a fish oil tablet or linseed/flaxseed oil capsule if you are vegetarian. There is also a known link between the state of the gut and some depression.[3] A great way to make sure your children's tummies are full of healthy bacteria is to give them some natural yoghurt or bio-yoghurt every day or just a probiotic pill. They could have fun growing their own yoghurt, which is cheap and easy to do.

Time management

Time management is a great behavioural tool to help you make changes in your life. Do not underestimate the power of a time management sheet to solve some of your life problems.

Using a time management sheet (there are plenty available on the internet), make a new plan that takes into account all the special things you want to do to enhance your communication and interaction at home. Put in time for downtime with the children, downtime for you, exercise and talking time. You can also extend your sleep time, plan your holidays and generally help yourself to feel in control of your life again, making sure that you are not 'overbooking' on activities or wasting time that is precious. Give children a time management sheet to make their own daily plan so they are learning to take some responsibility for time management.

Start to draw awareness to states of mind

Start to talk with your children, your partner and loved ones about states of mind that are easy to work with. You could start a technique or activity for times when the family are together, such as dinner time. Perhaps ask, 'What are you grateful for today?' This will give children a chance to think about their thinking and start to talk about acceptance and gratitude. You could then draw attention to more difficult states: 'What has been the hardest thing for you today?' My family used to tease me when I started to use these techniques but they secretly really enjoyed it and at least it gave them a chance to have fun as well as practice in speaking their mind. Gradually I noticed that if I did not ask the question they would wonder where our 'Where are you at?' questions were that day.

Dealing with life's normal ups and downs

We cannot, and perhaps should not try to, defend our children from the normal ups and downs of life. It is inevitable that your child will face challenges. Falling out with friends at school, struggling with a new piece of learning, coming last on sports day are all part of the important drama of a child's life — not to be dismissed but to be learnt from. These types of experiences will not adversely affect your child's mental health or create low self-esteem. I would call these healthy challenges that are developmental and normal, challenges that offer your child an opportunity to learn and grow and require your attention, support and teaching. Helping your child navigate these challenges is a serious part of mind-minded parenting.

Then there are challenges that are slightly more demanding on a child, that make them feel more seriously upset and nervous. These challenges will require attention, support and more consideration from parents and may even include support from school. These are challenges such as parents getting divorced, moving house, a sick parent or grandparent, mental health problems or addiction problems for the parent. In these cases you'll know why your child is struggling and, hopefully, what to do about it. It will take time and patience to settle their nervousness and the stress that this puts on them. These challenges are about emotional wellbeing and your enduring love for your child.

Depression, anxiety and self-harm in children and teens

There are scenarios where you do not really know what is going on for your child and you do not know why they are behaving the way they are. They are baffling, bewildering and you do not know where to start. These could be challenges for your child that have developed over time without you noticing, or it could be that you thought they were not unusual until someone brought it to your attention.

A most common scenario is when a parent discovers their child is self-harming. The usual response is to panic, which we have already established is normal but is not going to help. If this is the challenge that you currently face, don't start to blame yourself or others. The issue is likely to be a result of a combination of factors such as hurt in relationships, fear of failing, stress or bullying. It might also be added to by your child's temperament or genetic disposition, a developmental shift such as puberty or moving class and the child's need for support and new learning. Once you have raised the subject with your child, it may be helpful to get advice from a professional, such as your doctor or school counsellor, if your child is getting out of control in some way and you do not know what is going on for them. You can also just continue to reassure, discuss, watch and observe and see if you can gradually see what is happening, telling your child that you need to keep them safe and that there are risks with self-harm as a technique for reducing anxiety and that other techniques may be more effective. These days self-harm is a way for young people to relieve themselves from stress and upset, and they tell us it takes their mind off mental pain and worry. It causes great worry to parents but perhaps this might be an intended consequence, with a child showing, in fact, how worried they are about some unspoken matter.

How to help your child

Depression and anxiety are close partners and more often than not an anxious and more sensitive child will be prone to depression about things over which they have no control. Children can try so hard to cope and then fall into despair, collapsing into depression when they realize they can never change the things they may have been trying to control.

All the things mentioned earlier that enhance wellbeing can be gathered in preparation to help children with more complex states of mind, if and when there has become a risk of a more serious mental health problem such as depression. Here, as an example, is a plan to help you understand and help a child with depression (as opposed to just normal ups and downs).

1. Try to understand their thoughts and feelings. Take some time to reflect on what might be happening from their perspective. Think about how it is to be in their shoes right now so that you can start with empathy, compassion and imagination rather than judgment.

2. Particularly focus on trying to understand any issue about which they feel helpless.

3. Talk with them and help them resolve issues that are troubling them.

4. Look at the situation as a family rather than focusing on the child.

5. Help the child engage in experiences that create positive affect and mood.

6. Check their diet and ensure it is healthy (see p. 111 on food and mood).

7. Monitor their sleep patterns.

8. Arrange a health check with their doctor and get advice on further assessment.

9. Spend more time with your child in order to reassure them and tune in to their state of mind.

10. Explain that self-harm can be a risk, with infections and even cutting a vein accidentally. Tell the young person you will have to remove dangerous objects from them if they endanger themselves. Encourage discussion on other forms of alleviating stress, especially talking about their worries.

11. Focus more on alternatives to cutting and self-harm than on the self-harm itself. Don't judge it … just help the young person see that there are other ways through.

It can be baffling to parents to find that they have a depressed child, particularly if they are parents who are trying hard, working hard and doing their best. It may seem as if there is some elusive quality they cannot quite grasp that is affecting their child. This quality will lie in the child's thinking and the emotions associated with these thoughts, and this is what you have to try to tackle with your child. What thoughts are worrying them most? What are they most sad about? What are they most frightened about? Is there anything making them happy?

It does not take money to help a child with depression, but it does take time and that might inadvertently cost you money. If you are a busy working parent you might have to take some time out from work to spend with your child in order to show them you are focusing on the problem. I have previously encouraged parents to take a month off and really get close to the problematic burden that their child is carrying. As a parent, you really need time to think in order to take on this burden and show your child that you will share it. I hope that you have an employer who will let you do this, but for many parents taking time off without leave is just too costly. Either way, sit down (with your partner if you have one or a helpful person if you don't) and make a plan that includes time for this child.

There are many subtle things that make children feel a little bit different and a little bit anxious. It could be your child's performance at school that is causing them anxiety that they cannot resolve. As a minimum, I would take time out to ask the child's teacher for at least half an hour of their time so that they can highlight any problems — social, emotional or learning — that are emerging at school. These include not just performance problems but issues with bullying, social integration, racism or rejection. It may be helpful to ask for an educational psychology assessment that helps you to understand any learning difficulties your child could have that are causing them unresolvable stress or anxiety. It is very easy for learning difficulties to go undetected, so that a child or young person feels different, anxious, awkward or as if they are failing.

In creating a conversation with your child you will learn that even the most minute problem to them needs to be of importance to you. A child may not tell you about a problem or articulate the issue if they don't feel you can cope with it. Children frequently love their parents so much that they protect them from material that is difficult. On the other hand, if parents show they cannot cope with emotional material, children will also hide it. School counsellors are a very important resource for any child with depression, and can be very supportive with helping children talk in a more neutral way about their attachment relationships or anything that is bothering them. Child counsellors are often trained to use art or creative play with children so that they can show what it is that is causing them worry.

Alternatively, a child might not be able to manage their behaviour in class and this could make them unpopular with peers and make them feel angry and depressed. A teacher should be able to tell you if classroom behaviour is a problem, and you can get children assessed for ADHD or impulsivity that can often need managing. A doctor can make a referral for any appropriate assessments if this is the case. It is advisable anyway to visit your doctor and check any physical symptoms that a child or young person may have that may be causing them depression — a poor diet, low iron and viruses can cause a child or young person to feel physically depleted and very low, and you should let your doctor know anyway if your child is depressed so that they can advise on any local services that can assist you. Often, mental health services for children have long waiting lists for treating anxiety and depression because it is so common. While all of the suggestions in this book are based on sound evidence for treating children, it should not replace any medical treatment that is advised.

▼ ▼ ▼

You have a task of enquiry on your hands with a depressed child so that you can understand their situation more fully. Once your understanding can be employed to help with their real issues you will see a noticeable difference. Once this is in place, it is important to help them rebalance their system by attention to joyful events in their lives. This does not mean spoiling them. It could mean very simple things such as being read to, more walking and more age-appropriate play or even time cooking together. None of this has to cost money, but that play may have to be with you and this is why you might need more time.

It could be that your child's or teenager's state is a reflection of your own depression or despair and you might need time to talk this over with a supportive figure who has time for you. Many parents feel under pressure with work and financial demands to keep a home running and they are walking around exhausted and worried. They don't notice that their connection with their child is lessening or that the joy is seeping out of their family life and affecting their children. It is also the case that in younger children childhood depression is quite hard to detect and it is hard to access a younger child's thinking. In this case the depression will show in behavioural difficulties, such as not eating, and withdrawal. The changes that need to be made with these younger children most often relate to supporting them by taking time with them.

This is the kind of straightforward thinking that can help parents to support their children of any age through periods of adversity. It can also be used to help with the most common childhood mental health problems: separation anxiety, panic attacks and social phobia, obsessive compulsive tendencies and anxiety and depression, often resulting in self-harm or suicidal ideation. Separation anxiety relates to your child's need to keep you close. It means they worry about what will happen to you or them if you are separated. Panic attacks occur when anxiety has got beyond control and spirals into panic, which includes breathlessness and a sense of being overwhelmed. Social phobia arises when children, especially teenagers, are afraid of being judged by other people in social settings. They are very anxious about not feeling good enough and don't want to be seen by others, and this can be triggered by teasing and meanness at school. Obsessive compulsive tendencies are all about children worrying that they do things properly and get things right. Anxiety and depression are the net result of worried thoughts and lack of solution to problems. All of these require, as a basis, a conversation about issues that are worrying the child so that parents engage in planning that supports their child and helps them to calm down and feel understood. In most cases, if a child visits mental health services with any of the above conditions, a therapist would be assigned for a number of sessions to help parents to understand what is upsetting the child and make a plan to support them.

Much of the information in this book is geared to help you to begin to do that but again it is not a substitute for medical intervention. While most of these states can be addressed very simply through meaningful conversations and thoughtful attention to the detail of a child's life, especially the thoughts in your child's mind, it is very important to seek professional help immediately should your child exhibit suicidal thoughts or tendencies.

◢◢◢

In conclusion

In this chapter we have looked at the way that carers can plan to support children with their mental health and wellbeing. We have applied this to an example of childhood depression or self-harm in a teenager and also thought about helping with social phobia, separation anxiety, obsessive compulsive tendencies, anxiety and depression and panic attacks, which are the most common childhood mental health presentations. In doing this I have hopefully helped to demystify and take the anxiety and confusion out of some of these conditions.

There is plenty that parents can do to support children at these times. Unfortunately, they often have little information and feel that they can do nothing but wait helplessly in long queues for mental health services. There is plenty that can be done in the meantime, remembering the principles of Mind Kind parenting. Understanding your child's thoughts, feelings and behaviours will help them to feel more secure, and more information will help you to achieve this. Kind and supportive responses will go a long way to making your child feel better (which is what you really want as a parent).

The main message of this chapter is: when your child is going through a period of difficulty and change that causes them anxiety, what they really need is your support and understanding. So don't ever give up on trying to understand and show your child that you are confident they can soon feel better.

Parenting errors

Over time I have had plenty of opportunity to observe parents who are doing a good job of keeping children safe and feeling loved, not realizing that their parenting is Mind Kind. Other parents have been unaware of risk factors in parenting and have genuinely not been educated to realize the consequences of risky behaviours that could upset the balance of a child's mind and affect their mental health. It is clear that there are definite risk factors that could lead to difficulties for your child; some of these are due to challenges arising in life and some are through abusive and neglectful behaviours. I think it's helpful to differentiate between life events that inevitably occur and raise risk levels, and behaviours that dramatically raise risk levels.

Life events that raise risk

Ill health, mental illness, death, divorce, traumatic incidents such as car accidents, outbreak of war, famine, poverty, sudden accidents, natural disasters such as flood or earthquake, unemployment and redundancy are examples of life events that can't be helped but cause parents and their children to be seriously upset, depressed and anxious or even traumatized. Essentially these events can happen to literally anyone. It is important to support and encourage carers to try to stay in control of their parenting at these times, for their children. It may be hard to achieve. If parents are so overwhelmed by their circumstances it will give the children a sense that no one is in control of them and this will frighten them. However, if parents can in some way separate off their distress at these times and manage it in a thoughtful way, they may be able to put a reassuring aspect of their personality to one side to provide some reassurance for their child. It is an important time for grandparents and friends and relatives or people in the close community to step in and offer support. If close family are not available or are indeed unhelpful it is a time to ask for help from charities, schools, religious institutions and community services who may be able to offer resources. We live in a world of people who want to help.

Behaviours that raise risk

In my view, these include chosen behaviours such as drug addiction, alcohol addiction and parental conflict. I know that parents who are addicted to drugs and alcohol will not feel that they have a choice about that addiction. This may be true but it is definitely true that it is hard to recover from addiction without support. But parents have to find a way to manage how they behave during that addiction around their children. There are, of course, arguable points in between, so while divorce is often not preventable it is certainly true that parental conflict around children is 100 per cent preventable. If children are being raised in a war zone, parents can hardly be held responsible for the trauma that is caused to those children and they just need support to get them out and protect them as much as possible. As a society we have a duty to support those in this kind of life scenario and we cannot avoid these realities. But those instances are very different from the situations where dangerous experiences for children arise when conflicted parents unwittingly place their children in their very own war zone in their homes.

Ultimately, all of these risk factors, both behavioural and life events, require management of the environment around children. All children have risk factors around them and while some parents need to be more aware of what that looks or feels like, most parents are managing and assessing this all the time in quiet ways. Equally, children may have protective factors around them like supportive grandparents or extended family. The work of Michael Rutter, described as 'the father of child psychology', points out that exposure to three risk factors (i.e. drugs, domestic violence or alcohol) could lead to a 75 per cent possibility of the development of a behavioural difficulty in a child, whereas the presence of a loving and supportive parent could undoubtedly reduce risk.

Parenting errors, parenting mishaps and good enough parenting

In my work I have been able to observe not only what families get right for their children but also what families get wrong. I have seen the extreme end of gross parental behaviour leading to removal of children from the home.

I have also observed happy households where children are contented and secure because parents have their minds on the task of parenting and are able to manage life around and for their children, and enjoy engaging in the task. The homes that provide sufficient parenting are not perfect households where everything goes right all the time and nobody ever has any problems. But they can be defined as households where there is sufficient attention to important issues in a child's life. I refer to this as mindful parenting. This is also Mind Kind parenting, which not only cares for children, but also facilitates their wellbeing in a conscious and thoughtful way as well acknowledging that children have minds of their own.

This chapter will give you enough information about extreme mistakes as well as 'good-enough' parenting, and you will be able to judge for yourself where you need to make changes or, better still, where you need to validate your current parenting. The amazing thing about parenting is that you can change your tendencies and habits as soon as you like.

The following are examples of common parenting errors.

Slapping

Do not use slapping for any purpose whatsoever during parenting. Only children who do not know how to behave and solve their problems can be forgiven for engaging in slapping. Slapping is an ineffective reaction that simply makes children feel upset and angry and affects their developing personality. Children who are slapped feel misunderstood by their parents and in the long term they never really forgive their parents for slapping them. I have sat through hours of interviews with parents who recall being slapped as children. As adults they are still hurting and confused.

If you are a parent who slaps, you are getting something wrong and you are not thinking clearly about your behavioural responses. If you are annoyed or upset by your child's behaviour you can tell them this and tell them which behaviour you would like to see — but slapping only means, in a child's view, that you hate them momentarily and disregard their feelings. It also shows that you are not able to articulate problems and that, like a child, you are acting them out through behaviour. Stop now — and find another way to relate to your child. You probably don't realize the consequences of slapping, but you are choosing the wrong way to help your child understand behaviour.

Drug and alcohol problems

Your drug and alcohol addiction may have run out of control and there may have been difficult circumstances leading to your dependence on substances. This book will not judge you for that. Many very loving parents have drug and alcohol addictions. But many of these parents do not realize the consequences of their addictive behaviour on their child. In my view, there are two choices. First, you could manage your addiction in a very conscious way so that it affects your child as little as possible. However, 'addiction' and 'consciousness' are contradictory. Second, try to beat the addictive behaviour through rehabilitation, support, counselling, medical advice and general life changes. There are plenty of charities who do amazing work with helping people to beat addiction for free and you can be released from the torment of addictive behaviour.

If you are drinking and drunk around your child, you are a danger to them and your behaviour will confuse them. They will be frightened of you as they cannot predict what you might do next. In addition, you might be spending money on alcohol that is needed for them. It is very difficult to hide the fact that you have an alcohol abuse problem — everyone will know even if they pretend they don't. Drug abuse may be a little easier to hide but this won't make it any better for you. Plenty of parents do parent through drug addiction and this can be achieved if they choose to prioritize their child's needs, run a well-organized and orderly home, keep drug dealers away from their home, don't use money for feeding and clothing children on drugs and be discrete about times of using. This is a tall order but parents can do this.

Ideally, discuss with someone how you can beat your problem or gradually decrease your intake of drugs and alcohol. You might want to reflect with a counsellor on the causes of your problem, because there will be root causes in your thinking. You are also likely to increase your child's chances of addiction if they observe your lifestyle and make it their own.

Domestic violence

If partners resort to slapping, hitting, shouting, threatening, psychological control, deprivation and emotional abuse with each other, they might like to be aware that this is the same as directly abusing their children. When children observe domestic violence between adults they will be afraid and their nervous systems will be alerted when they see a parent being hurt (a parent to whom they are attached and love dearly) in the same way as if they were being hurt themselves. The outcomes are poor for children in terms of mental health, anxiety and depression, particularly in later years. So you might think you have got away with violence because your children are little and therefore unaware and unable to make sense of what is happening. But they store this alarming information in their long-term memory and it affects their regulatory and emotional systems, and often affects their future relationships.

There are plenty of resources for both women and men who may be entrapped in violent relationships. Every local authority will have an affiliated organization to help deal with domestic violence. While it is a hard and fearful thing to break away from this kind of relationship, it is what you will have to do for the safety and wellbeing of your children. Many people stay entrapped because they love their partner and live in the hope it will stop. If violence has been going on for even a very short time it is unlikely to stop, unless you do something very assertive about it and unless the perpetrator is willing to seek help. The messages from research are very clear: domestic violence affects the mental health and wellbeing of your child even if the child is very quiet about it.

Exposing your child to dangerous people

Unfortunately, some dangerous people are adept at spotting and preying on vulnerable single parents (men or women) so that they can gain access to their children. It can be hard to recognize this when you are a vulnerable parent in need of a partner and this is uncomfortable reading, but women and men do have to be cautious about inviting complete strangers into their lives for romantic or even just supportive interaction. If you don't know who you are getting and you don't know about their background, you could be putting your child at risk, so it is wiser to be cautious in the early stages of a new relationship about who you are inviting into the lives of your children.

Poor choice of words with children and emotional abuse

The three points above relating to drugs and alcohol, slapping and wrong choice of partner are categorical. They fall into the clear category of 'do not do this'. Emotional abuse, though, is hard to identify and parents are often surprised that they are pulled up on the way they talk to their children. Here is where the clear rules end and the Mind Kind rules set in.

Mind Kind is about seeing every single word you speak to your child as an opportunity to help them with their lives. Occasionally you might yell and you will have your own bad moods and difficult scenarios to deal with. But the rule is not to take your frustrations out on your children. Tell them you are dealing with something difficult and need some time. It's likely that your problems have very little to do with them. If you have tiny children and you are dealing with something difficult, see if you can get someone to give you a few hours of respite so that you can put your mind to rights with a good plan, or walk with the stroller to clear your head or get someone to help you to move forward mentally and emotionally. Either way, do not take out your unhappy distress on your children — it is an emotionally abusive act and it will confuse them.

Assuming you feel well and are coping, then there is the matter of ordinary life. It is surprising the number of very caring parents I meet who use inappropriate language about their children, and I don't mean swear words. Here are just a few: 'He's a pain in the backside', 'She's a devil', 'He's evil', 'I'll punch your lights out if you do that', 'You miserable kid', 'You are stupid', 'Greedy little pig', 'You're hopeless', 'You don't have a brain between you'. Do not dismiss the power of these words and the effect they have on your children. All of these statements are emotionally abusive, in that they make your child feel bad or unhappy; they are words that reject your child and show a lack of acceptance and validation. The words you use with your child will seriously affect their self-esteem and the way they view themselves. You can choose them to be kind and accurate or thoughtless and meaningless. If you were called words as a child, you might think this is a normal part of parenting or even affectionate. It is not. Your words deeply affect your child's brain.

I am very concerned about emotional abuse and the impact it has on children. I am concerned about parents who are unaware of the words they use in front of their children and behind their backs. If you want to let off steam about your child, do it somewhere where they cannot hear you. When you have dealt with your emotions and are feeling more balanced, if there is something bothering you about your child then either make a plan to help them with that or talk to someone about your concerns who can help you to restructure your thinking.

Trying to get a psychiatric label for your child

I meet parents who need support, understanding and help with determining whether a child has a mental health disorder when in fact they may not realize that their parenting is probably seriously affecting their child's thinking and behaviour. Sometimes there is good cause for concern about a child's presentation and I don't wish to invalidate the real concerns of parents. Autism is a typical example where a child can display very confusing behaviours that require assessment and parents need a lot of reassurance. However, there are parents who will not accept that their child does not have a disorder such as ADHD, autism, manic depression or psychosis. They continually return to services to have their child assessed for these disorders in the face of being told that they simply need to find ways to manage their child's behaviour. They are left continuously anxious about the causes of their child's difficulties and nobody has taken the time to explain the links between relationship and behaviour to them. These are parents who find it hard to imagine that their own behaviour is affecting their child, and who need a lot of help with understanding the causes of their child's behavioural distress.

I am not parent blaming. Parents are often confused and demoralized by these issues, and exhausted if children are difficult. Parents in this situation need genuine support and time to help them understand what is happening in their relationship with their child. Professionals need to intervene in a helpful and supportive way when parents present in this way. They need to either eliminate the possibility of conditions by proper assessment or get on with helping the parent understand the dynamics of what is going on.

Rigid parenting

This is parenting where parents love their children, but their style of parenting does not account for the mental and emotional life of their child. They simply expect that what should be done should be done now, with no discussion or reflection whatsoever. It could be referred to as a 'my way or the highway' style of parenting. The rules are the rules and parents of this style get rather exasperated if their children show any sign of avoidance.

Unfortunately, this kind of parenting creates avoidant strategies in children, and since there is no room for discussion, children will do the minimum that they can to give the parent what they want. Parents who employ this strategy tend to be rather angry parents who get frustrated that they do not get what they want out of their child in terms of behaviour. In these kinds of households there is no room to breathe, no free thought and children will start to show you their dissent or avoid you rather than discuss their thoughts and feelings. Rigid parenting rather squeezes the joy out of being a child. The good thing about these households is that they will probably be organized, there will be a good timetable and structure, and kids meet expectations. Children will get to school and schoolwork may be given priority over emotional lives.

If you fall into this category fear not, as there will be plenty you are getting right. You are showing your children that you value structure and organization and that you can get things done. But you won't be showing them the other side of their experience, in emotion, time and flexibility. So you may want to look at this. Here is the kind of behaviour we can see in highly rigid parenting:

» a tendency to undervalue warmth in the parental relationship

» a lack of child centredness

» being highly demanding of children

» an authoritarian style

» critical tendencies if the child gets things wrong.

Unfortunately, these behaviours may give you an immediate result but in the long term they will cause damage. Critical parents tend to produce rebellious children who are rather angry about life and sometimes they can become spiteful and angry towards other children, demonstrating exactly the kind of behaviours they are experiencing and internalizing. I have even seen children become ill and hypochondriacal as a way of dealing with this type of parenting, defending themselves from the high expectations of parents who simply make them feel bad, inadequate and anxious. Children can also start to fear failure as they know they are about to be criticized and they can be secretly angry, resentful and frustrated. This can lead them to become unhappy and not emotionally open enough to talk about their problems and resolve them. They also lack the ability to think for themselves.

Parents with this style might like to think about this impact and areas where they can soften up a little. Ask yourself if you have internalized this type of parenting from your own childhood. If the answer is yes, think about how that made you feel, if indeed you can remember and were allowed to know how you were feeling. You can discuss this parenting style with your partner and decide on strategies that could help you to change.

There are extraordinary small changes you can make that will make a big difference, such as the suggestions below.

Aim to praise more than criticize

Take a day and notice how many times you criticize in that day. Then take another day and see if you can find more reasons to praise your child than to criticize them. Instead of criticizing you can give helpful feedback on what could be different.

Try to examine areas of flexibility

See if there are areas where you can be flexible. For instance, I knew one quite rigid parent who became a parenting goddess when in the swimming pool with her children. Suddenly she was full of smiles and fun. Primarily this was because her physical and mental positioning shifted when in the water, so she turned from a tiger shark parent into a dolphin. Not surprisingly, her children were rather fond of swimming. So if it's hard to flex, see if there is one area where you can be more your 'other self'. Does it take kicking a ball around the garden with the kids or even watching a film with them? Either way, there is a softer, flexible parent in there just dying to get out for some joy with your children.

Is your timetable making you rigid?

A lot of parents today become more rigid, I think, under the pressure of working life and their timetable. Some people who may only be moderately rigid in nature become obsessional rigidity monsters due to the pressure they are under. If this is so, then take a spacious and compassionate look at yourself. I don't blame parents for erring this way. I could tend towards this way myself at times and, let's be real, sometimes even an army sergeant would be hard pressed to squeeze kids into the timetable of the average school week. See if you can just make one day a week a day in which you can ease up and relax the rules — see what happens with a no timetable day and let the children talk with you a little more. That would be a brilliant start.

Lax, excessively liberal parenting

All of you who thought that the rigid parents were getting it wrong can now look at the flipside of this kind of parenting. That is, an overly lax and liberal style of parenting that has no rules, believes that kids will find their own way in life and cannot see what the problem about parenting is. In my years of observation of parents, this style includes parents who let their kids smoke marijuana in the home, who drink with their kids, and parents who think of their kids as their best friends. Conversely, there are children with parents like this who are fending for themselves with no parental support whatsoever. And there are a whole range of questionable activities in between such as parents who sunbathe nude and think their kids are not bothered, parents who go to music festivals and give their young kids (under the age of ten) completely free rein to do what they like, parents who think it's okay to let kids watch X-rated movies that might seriously affect them. Sadly, onwards down the spectrum there are parents who exploit their children into criminal behaviour and activity in a complete state of blindness to the authority and morality that is needed to be a parent.

Children at this end of the spectrum are likely to receive more positive attention and affection from their parents, but they may also have no sense of boundaries and this can make them paranoid, insecure and frightened. It will also leave them with an excessive amount of responsibility that they have to shoulder on their own, potentially producing over-anxious and over-burdened children, or alternatively children who give up and just become antisocial.

There will be occasions in healthy parenting when the barriers get let down and parents have lax days and even lapses, but this should not be the norm. Parents who are significantly lax and forgetful of their responsibilities are forgetting that parenting is a task, a job and a role, and they let their children down. They need to spend a weekend corresponding with their rigid parenting counterparts, who could teach them something about rules and responsibility. The rule goes like this: someone somewhere in a family is going to have to be responsible for management. Make sure it is you or your partner who is doing that — and not your children.

Here is the basic set of Mind Kind values:

» Children need someone to be in charge and in control.

» Children need to differentiate between the role of child and the role of adult.

» Routine and predictability are very good for children.

» Children like rules; they help them know where they are and feel safe.

» Children need your attention.

» Parenting is not an optional game.

Misattribution and blame

This is where parents react and blame their children for things they have not done, or blame them for things they have done but could not help. It is also where parents name the wrong emotional state in their child, such as telling the child they were jealous when in fact they were struggling with deep feelings about sharing, or naming the child as angry when in fact they were trying to deal with some sense of unfairness in their life. These behaviours are easy enough to mistake when a parent is stressed, but these mistakes can and should be corrected. It is hard to have no power and have someone tell you that you have done or thought something you have not. For a child this is confusing. Imagine your boss coming to you and saying, 'You're a troublemaker' because you have joined a union. This would be unjust and worthy of complaint. We have to be careful about our judgments of anybody but we have to ameliorate our harsh thoughts about a child's behaviour in order to help them accept and discuss this with you. If this behaviour is constant from a parent, it counts as emotional abuse as discussed above.

Tiger or pussycat?

There is a difference between maintaining realistic expectations and aspirations for your child's development and future, and simply having expectations that are too high. It is all a matter of parental evaluation and parental reflection.

First of all, take a look at what it is you expect your child to achieve and check carefully that there is a reality principle in there that will protect your child from an overwhelming sense of failure. Don't push your child to be a footballer if, in fact, they show an inclination towards art and drama, and check carefully with your child what their own aims and aspirations are. As we see in the section on child development, what this is ultimately doing is not accepting your child for who they really are. So lots of questions need to be asked when you are behaving like a tiger parent, pushing your kids forward and thinking constantly of their success. Did you get to be who you really are? Did you fulfil your own aspirations?

You also have to employ your Mind Kind thinking because it is highly likely that children with this kind of parent will be vulnerable to obsessive compulsive tendencies and anxiety. They will be anxious and afraid of failure and unable to live with the reality that everybody fails sometime, that we can't be good at everything and we can learn so much from mistakes. On the other hand, I think there is no harm in listening to and corralling and capitalizing on children's realistic expectations of themselves. No goal is too impossible for a child between the age of six and adulthood. With parental support and advice, this may be tempered slightly with a reasonable plan for development. It is, for example, not improbable that any average six-year-old in the current time could acquire the skills (over the following twenty years) to get him or her on a flight to Mars in the future if that is what they really want. So start planning now if this is what your child aspires to do, but make time for downtime and other non-doing activities such as relaxation. He or she will be on that spacecraft to Mars for a long time, just waiting around, and a tendency to anxiety will not help them.

Lack of aspirations

The opposite of pushing children too hard is not having any aspirations for them at all. What a waste of a parenting opportunity and a failure to notice the process of life and evolution to have no goals for your children, to not wish them a future or to move forward. Even the smallest goal will be good enough to be interested in — a child's collection of cars, their Lego building, their stamp collection, their love of fashion, dance, a sport, drama, craft or planes. Here is an example: one totally inept father that I once knew became a hero overnight for his child, who wished to be an airline pilot, when he took him plane spotting on the roof of the car park at the nearest city airport. They started to love their time together on that roof and it was a symbol of the rest of that child's life. That same young person has probably flown you on an international flight by now.

It is never too late to get interested, and where your child's interests lie is where their heart is.

Constant activity

Almost every family I meet, with the exception of those who are not engaging well with their children, seems to face the problem of life today: doing too much. On the face of it one might wonder why this is a problem. Parents think they are being great parents for their children when they are engaging in meaningful activities and they are right. But there are some things to evaluate here. First, ask yourself: where and when does your child have some downtime? By downtime I refer to the idea that they are under no pressure to conform, having nothing on their timetable and can just relax or rest and breathe and allow their mind to wander. For rigid parenting types it is common that they do not monitor the way their child is using their energy and do not make allowances for the need for rest and recuperation in order to restore functioning. When energy levels take a dive (which they do in any normal human being) there is a need for time to restore. The net result of not taking time out is that children (and adults) can become irritable, anxious, depressed and generally unhappy and unable to make sense of anything. For example, this is often the case for children at the end of a school day.

The concept of downtime in terms of brain restoration, self-regulation and wellbeing is now prevalent within the neuroscientific field. For example, Dan Siegel talks about downtime as being part of a daily routine for children that helps them regulate their brain and their system.[1] I think it is part of being a well-regulated person, giving your brain a chance to think more deeply. When the body is resting, even just for twenty minutes in one day (preferably twice) then the brain becomes more effective. For children, this gives them a chance to find deep solutions to the small problems they have, and a chance for integration between mind and body as well as the various regions of the brain. It also gives children a chance to reflect and be with themselves. This helps them not only respect themselves but also respect these needs in others.

I know that constant activity ticks a lot of boxes on good parenting but downtime also ticks the boxes on sensitively attuned parenting. Which sort of parent do you want to be? You can have really successful children who know how to manage their energy levels and as a consequence have increased wellbeing and very probably increased achievement.

When children have too much power

I think it is very beneficial that our world has evolved so much that we treasure and value children as individuals. We take children's rights very seriously. UNICEF have a Charter for Children's Rights which I reproduced with their kind permission in my last book, *Mindful Therapeutic Care for Children: A guide to reflective practice.*[2] As a society, we are more mindful of the voice of children and Britain's *Children Act 2004* incorporates the values of giving credence to the voice and wishes of children who can speak up for themselves. Generally, we may think of children over the age of seven as being able to speak their mind on what they think and feel, although this age is not set in stone.

Small children will indicate clearly what they want and we cannot ignore their communications to us through their behaviour. Despite this, there can be problems in families where the balance of power is given over to children in an inappropriate proportion to their age; I see this in increasing frequency in families and some institutions. Again, there is a balance to find between the two extremes of disempowering and disenabling children, and allowing them so much power that they are likely to destroy both themselves and their family. The problem with children having too much power is that they are not happy with it. The other problem is that children will always instinctively make bids for as much power as they can get. This has to be understood in order to understand power in children. It is natural for them to want more from you and to increase their strength, because nature gives children a survival instinct that says they should gain as much as possible — they are born to maximize the responses they get from parents. However, children who are given everything they want and who are given too much power and control simply become lost, in their demeanour, in their homes and in their minds, because they are not given limits.

How much power you give to your children at any age will depend very much on how you organize power dynamics in your own life. If you are a nervous person and passive in your approach to life, you have to be careful that you do not convey this to children, who then feel they have to take over and take control. In the same way, if you are too lax in your control and management your children may feel they have to take control. Generally, parents who are ineffective in their management find that children will take up the power vacuum in the family and fill it for themselves. As a result, they might become stressed and over-burdened with the responsibility of this. This is not an opportunity for parent bashing and there is no point in making yourself feel a failure if you have a child who has taken over and is bossing you around, calling the shots and generally showing themselves to be burdened by being the boss. Start by reflecting on what is happening. Look for the telltale signs — who is in charge of the daily plan? Who is in charge of pocket money? Who is in charge of activities? Who organizes, supports and liaises with school? Is it you? It needs to be.

If you think you are a disempowered parent, look at some assertiveness training, which is enormously helpful in teaching people to understand the general principles of healthy interaction and communication. There are a lot of great books on the subject. A counsellor or therapist can also help you to develop your communication style, or your partner might support you to be more assertive. Do not be downhearted; there are many things that can be done to counteract a child with too much power. They won't like it at first but will soon adapt to the new power dynamics in the home and be more contented. I can recommend *The Mental Health Handbook* (third edition) by Trevor Powell, which has a great module on assertive communication.

Misjudging ability

This is an area where thoughtful accuracy is needed. While it is fully understandable that every parent should wish to have their child be the greatest and the best at everything, it is very uncomfortable for children when their abilities are misread and parents are misattuned to their real ability.

Don't imagine how things are — check out how things actually are. This includes a look at sports, music and all the subjects in which your child engages. There is a very real case for supporting and developing weakness and encouraging and enhancing strength. So if a child adores their art then do everything to progress their skill, ability and creativity. If a child detests sport do not force them to aim for sports personality of the year. It is wasted energy. Simply encourage them to invest in just enough exercise for fitness and health, and allow them to indulge in who they really are.

Of course, children need to try out new things, as do adults. We may well think we hate a particular sport or activity and we can certainly make a good judgment call once we have given it a try. But I think it is a fundamental waste of psychic energy to force children to do what they are never going to be good at — and for what reason? Always look to the balance of positives and negatives: a child may have a brilliant IQ and be top of the class at everything, but look out for where he or she needs support. Do they need help with their empathy, for example? Do they need support with sport?

One final thing to remember is to praise your children for the effort they have made rather than randomly tell them they are brilliant or clever. If you praise effort they will realize that hard work is the key to life regardless of the outcome. If you only tell them they are smart they will have an inflated ego and not even know why they are smart.

Arguing with your kids

I am always proud when parents I have worked with remember this rule. That is, if you ever find yourself arguing with your children, just remind yourself instantly that you have got it wrong. You are the adult. Feel free to discuss anything and everything with your children. Feel free to allow them to give you their views on anything and correct their information if you see fit. However, if you are arguing you have put yourself in the position of being a child and you are making a mistake. Take a break, remind yourself that there is only one person who makes the rules and reconsider your approach.

Your options are:

» remind your child of the rules and why they are there

» give your child time to think about the rules

» explain that you do not argue about the rules but that you are willing to take feedback and consider any valid information and if appropriate make changes

» tell your child you will get back to them and have a discussion when you have had time to reflect on what they have said.

The 'always an elephant in the room' parent

Some parents never talk about the things that clearly need to be spoken about. They can appear like lax and inept parents when in fact they are probably kind parents who don't like to upset their children with reality.

This is a problem because their children may give up on facing reality and start to live in a fantasy world since nobody helps them face real feelings.

These are well-meaning parents who are dismissive of emotion and real life in themselves. They seek to protect their children from reality by not talking about it or brushing it off easily — but in doing so, they take away their children's capability and strength to cope with reality. There could literally be an elephant in the room that does not get talked about, whereas mind-minded parents might tackle that elephant one bite at a time.

Not enough information

These parents may think that children can read their minds. This is similar to the type of parent above who has not yet fully understood that children are little information-processing machines. They process emotional, physical and chemical information from their body to their brains, needing information fed to them to increase this capacity in themselves and to evaluate their lives. So while it may seem banal, it is an advanced parenting skill to feed your children appropriate information on everyday things like the plan for the day, the menu for the day, the plan for the weekend, school letters and what is happening with the family. In return, children feed you information and you demonstrate to them your joy in dealing with this, in processing and thinking about things. You ask questions, you seek to understand the child's reality and you learn more about how your child is working. You give your child feedback on how you see them working and whether something worked for them. For example, you might discuss their school report in detail rather than just read and comment 'good' or 'bad' or 'well done'. That is not information processing, it is dismissing the report. Information feeding involves going through the report, pulling out comments and thinking about them. This shows children that information is valuable and shows them how to manage the information.

However, it is important to remember that information processing is not about an excessive amount of information that your child cannot handle. The information has to be relevant, age appropriate, safe and not disturbing in the way it is presented. It has to be presented in a fairly organized and well-processed fashion that has been thought through. In short, it should be presented in a mind-minded sort of way. So don't throw desperate, emotionally laden information at your children such as, 'We're broke this week and how are we going to pay the bills?' Instead, speak with your children on the same subject in an organized way that does not frighten them: 'We are going to have to budget carefully this week so I am going to be careful with the shopping. There is plenty to eat but let's think of what we can cut back on. Loads of families have to budget like this so let's see what we can do.' This is a Mind Kind conversation on life's complex information that gives your children an opportunity to learn.

Too much information

The flipside to parents who do not give their children enough information or narrative on life is the parent who gives their child too much information or narrative on their own lives. This is not an acceptable form of parenting and is quite likely to disturb your child, mainly because they will worry about you. Children are destined to pick up on the emotional states of their parents anyway and are psychologically built to read the signals of their loved ones.

There will, of course, be times when parents are struggling like mad with overwhelming events and they simply cannot organize the material that is happening for them. A typical example is when a parent is ill. Hopefully, under such circumstances there will be people around who can help to organize such an overwhelming piece of information for a child. For example, I observed the process of one amazing parent who nursed a partner with a terminal heart disease at home with a family of three children. That parent managed to complete the desperately difficult and emotional task of nursing and caring for the sick partner while at the same time protecting the children and helping them to process the very difficult information it presented to them. That parent also managed to cope with the partner dying in the home and still managed to sift some of the deep horrors of this so that the children could process it yet take a realistic part in it. It was hard enough to do all these things and very difficult and painful for the children, but they were shielded to some extent by a very mindful and competent parent who gave them just enough of the burden with which to cope and grow. She gets the Mind Kind medal.

These natural events are part of real lives. Other events such as poverty, loss of a job or broken relationships happen to just about all of us. Life has adversity written into the script; it is part of being a real human being. We are lucky if we get away with a few of the inevitable aspects of life — in many countries parents must protect children from war, famine or political disorganization.

What you should aim to avoid is being the type of parent who assumes that your child can cope with an adult reality, leaving the child to manage the whole gambit of human emotion all in one go. Children cannot do this, even if they tell you that they can. The kind of parent that does not make some attempt at a stance that sifts material for a child is not thinking about the mind of their child.

Role reversal

This is simply where the parent becomes the child and the child becomes the parent. There will be occasions when this occurs accidentally. For instance, if there is an accident in the home and the child rushes for the first aid box in order to help their parent, or if a parent is momentarily upset and their child wishes to comfort them. It is a natural instinct for a child to be concerned for their parent or carer, and a part of their human kindness that they want to help and support those they love the most. Accidents and upsets are bound to occur.

What I am talking about here is where a child takes over and is providing continuous support, sustenance and nurturing for their parent so that the parent can survive. In some ways in our society, this is behaviour that is almost sanctioned. We give awards to children who care for others. While I can see that this is wonderful for children who have shown extraordinary care, I do not think it is great to allow children to continuously be carers of adults. We do not live in the seventeenth century and we do not encourage child slavery (although sadly it is still perfectly legal in some countries). It is my committed view that children who are in a continuously caring role (i.e. cooking, cleaning and emotionally supporting parents or looking after other children) should be seen as children in need and social services and charities should look at the lives of children who are doing this so that they can support their families with relevant adults rather than have the children do this. (Such support involves help in the home — I'm not referring to putting children in care.) Parents cannot help it if they are extremely disabled or ill, but their children should still be given adult support.

For parents who feel that this may apply to them, this is not another chance to give yourself a beating; it is an opportunity to think about whether you can find emotional support from anywhere else. And to children all over the world who have no choice about taking up this caring role … we think of you.

Separation, divorce and step-parenting

I have given separation, divorce and re-formed families a chapter of their own because I believe this area needs special attention in terms of keeping children stable and understanding the effects on their emotional lives and mental health.

Statistics suggest that one in three families is a re-formed or blended family. There is nothing unusual about the formation of stepfamilies and it is not a modern phenomenon. Historically, stepfamilies have been the norm when you bear in mind the number of adults who would have died early or mothers who might have died in childbirth. One famous figure — Elizabeth I — had four stepmothers following the execution by her father, Henry VIII, of her own mother, Anne Boleyn, when she was two. Elizabeth was parented by Henry's four successive wives, and formed a particularly close bond with her fourth stepmother, Catherine Parr, who managed to outlive Henry and hang on to her head. During this period in history it was common for families to re-form and children had to get on with step-parents — little attention would have been given to whether the children actually liked it, or how it might affect their development and lives.

Unfortunately, we are saddled with a myth about the wickedness of step-parenting that has probably emerged out of the historical formation of stepfamilies and lack of attention to the challenges therein, meaning that all of the difficult material and emotion was transferred into rather dark projected stories about stepmothers and fathers, sisters and brothers. There is probably some foundation to this dark myth, but on the whole it is best to stick with the realities. This chapter is about those realities — let's look into the darkness.

Differences in stepfamilies

The fact is, there are many step-parents who struggle with their stepchildren. There are just as many stepchildren who struggle with their step-parents and choose to reject them. Some re-formed families exist as if there is a Mexican standoff between everyone and this can contribute to feelings being hurt on a long-term basis. In light of this it is also easy to see why second marriages break down due to stress and pressure. There is one basic ingredient within stepfamilies that causes these challenges and this can be encapsulated in the word 'difference'. The difference in styles of parenting and behaviour within families can be challenging. Such difference can be very enriching and life-enhancing if supported and facilitated in the right direction, and very destructive if not given enough attention.

Many parents enter into new relationships being completely blind to the issues of mind mindedness (i.e. what is going on in the minds of their children). They assume that because they are passionately in love, and perhaps even initially blinded with love for a person, that their children will feel that way too and will enjoy the ride. Often the opposite is true, and children do not enjoy the introduction of a new figure. Just as often, they initially accept the new figure and then challenges start to emerge as time goes by. But why does this fundamental instinct to reject have a chance to emerge so abruptly at these times? For the moment we are talking here about when stepfamilies take a difficult turn rather than when they are having a load of life-enhancing fun together and getting along well.

The answer to this very deep question can be found in attachment theory, which we discussed in Chapter 1. Attachment theory advises that children are born to stay close to one preferred figure or primary parent rather than a number of parental figures. Children can accept a small group of people to care for them such as grandparents, aunties, uncles or child minders. But with step-parents there is a difference in that they are not naturalistic to the child and usually unfamiliar. Initially this challenges the child's intrinsic and primitive urge: 'I have one mum and one dad and they are *mine*.' If we understand how children instinctively respond around their attachment figures, we cannot be surprised at the incredible power of this urge. This instinctive compulsion to possess a parent is there to assist their survival. If a parent dies, this instinct can be transferred on to another parent if they show sufficient love and sensitivity towards the child. This happens in scenarios of substitute parenting such as adoption, fostering or guardianship. However, even in these cases, the shadow or DNA of the primary parent does not get erased, because it is always there coursing through the veins of the child.

In situations of substitute parenting or step-parenting, this is a very hard truth that is frequently forgotten. Shocked adoptive parents can be devastated when their children reject them because they cannot let go of the sense that they do not belong. Equally, I see many step-parents who are shocked that children cannot accept them fully and wholeheartedly. Even when step-parents don't expect pride of place (and few are foolish enough to expect this) they still get 'put in their place' by children who wish them to know 'you are not mine — I belong to another'. This fundamental, primitive law of belonging runs through many of our life experiences and translates into many of our best-loved tales. The tragedy of Cathy and Heathcliff in Emily Brontë's *Wuthering Heights* is one example. Cathy and her adoptive brother Heathcliff became so bound together that neither of them could accept any other partner into their lives, with tragic consequences. Emily Brontë describes in this story the incredible power of fundamental love combined with the slightly psychopathic tendencies of the possessive Heathcliff.

Family dynamics and culture

Aside from this basic level of DNA and human attachment, there is another thick layer of difference that can be labelled 'family dynamics, style and culture'. The culture of one family may be fundamentally different to the culture and style of another. These dynamics and styles ultimately affect our thinking, our emerging identities and the adults we become. They are reflected in our behaviours, values, attitudes and the way we relate to people. One family might prize educational achievement, another might prize emotional support for one another and yet another could be materialistic and goal driven. Some children are used to parents who keep a distance and some children are used to close relationships. None of these is wrong, but we sometimes forget that children can feel as if they are living in an alien world when they come up against another culture. This alienation can persist and continue if the dynamics of the differences are not supported, respected, narrated and understood for children. This is not to say that competing families have to change their culture — because they do not — they simply have to be able to understand, identify and respect each other's differences.

How to position yourself as a step-parent

There are few rules on which we can rely in the arena of step-parenting but one of the clear messages to emerge is that it is not necessary for you to love your stepchild. If, as a starting point, you can accept, understand and respect the unique character of your stepchild and their different style of relating, you are far more likely to succeed as a step-parent. Our expectations are bound to be thwarted if we approach a stepchild with the view that we are a very important and authoritative person in their life. In fact, this is a stance that may cause some resistance from your stepchildren. If, on the other hand, you approach the 'task' with the view that you need time to understand who they are, and they need time to establish who you are and where they want to put you on their map of people in their mind, you stand far more chance of forming an alliance that is helpful, safe, rich in potential and fun, but most of all enduring. This is preferable to making assumptions about how things are going to be, followed by a clash of cultures and a breakdown in communication.

It is much better to be a respected figure who is seen as safe and unimposing than a passionately loved diva who is banished from the child's kingdom when they don't meet expectation. A child really does have the right to choose where they are going to put you in their map of people. If you get to be accepted and liked as even a minor figure, you will have done well. Don't expect to be loved and adored, and try to understand the reasons for that. You may have to get comfortable with coming second on this one.

Lowering your expectations and raising your Mind Kind skill

In light of what we have just discussed, it is far safer to come from a position of lowered expectation than to crash and burn on the first test flight with stepchildren. We must also remember that if we accept that children have the right to make up their own mind about a person, we really do have to accept their position. It is rather painful if a child, for whatever reason, decides that you are a person without status in their life and that they do not want you there. It is rather tough, but it is possible to live with this. It will not necessarily mean that you deserve that position (in fact, far from it) and that child's decision may be unfair to you. However, this book is about reality parenting and that includes reality step-parenting, so let's start with that fundamental reality — you are not liked and not accepted. How do you deal with that with grace, kindness and respect for the child and at the same time maintain your integrity, hold onto your sanity, keep your self-esteem and, most of all, not change the dynamics of the loving relationship in which you have chosen to be? It is going to be a painful love affair if you spend the rest of your relationship moaning about the stepchild who hates you. It will do nothing for your wellbeing and mental health and nothing for your relationship or your levels of happiness. I know there are a lot of step-parents who will have experienced being put in this position.

What to do as a step-parent

The first thing you need to do is absolutely nothing. Do not react to the child who decides you are not for them, do not get into the role that they might like you to be in — that of the wicked step-parent who is up to no good. There is only one person who should be trying to mediate this situation and that is your partner, who is presumably the parent of the child. They too need to accept their child's position and help them to understand more clearly the new situation with the step-parent and to allay any possible fears or anxieties about 'him/her taking over from my mum/dad'. But they are the most important person to also offer you support for your place in the heart of their child. The one thing you can expect and organize is understanding and reflection on the problems from the parent of the child who has put you in their child's life.

One family I worked with had a little girl of seven who pointed out to her stepfather rather quickly, 'My mum has always dealt with my discipline and

I don't want any from you.' The stepfather, concerned, became instantly sensitive to the fear that this little girl had about being cared for by a stepfather and he acceded to her request, responding, 'Of course ... I see ... that is absolutely fine.' That same stepfather did not go into a rage at being dismissed. He simply gracefully accepted the child's mindset and tried to understand why she should have such a strong reaction. On reflection, he found the child had had a rather difficult relationship with her own father and she therefore had to act quickly to keep herself safe. That same family is now an adult stepfamily, with the child now a young woman who has a very close relationship with her stepfather. He has never taken part in her discipline and has only been allowed to be in the position of a supporter to her mother. In this instance that acceptance and understanding worked very beautifully, but things are not always that easy and it took a lot of patience on the part of the stepfather and quite remarkable communication skills from the child.

In a more extreme case, a stepmother with whom I worked was rejected and summarily dismissed by her sixteen-year-old stepson, who tried to persuade his father to dump his new bride. It was not as if it was a hurried relationship. The father's wife had died after a prolonged illness and a year later he met his new partner. Two years later they got married, having taken every possible step to consider the feelings of a teenage boy who had lost his mother. There were many complicated dynamics in this situation, all of which the father and stepmother attempted to consider and take into consideration through family therapy and support. I am sad to say that there was no change whatsoever in the boy's attitude. By the time he was nineteen he continued to not only reject his stepmother but also to be oppositional and abusive to her. Eventually the father threw him out of the house as he would not tolerate this treatment, which he deemed to be unreasonable. The couple continued to try to reflect on the situation. They did not want the boy, now a young man, to feel rejected, but they felt they should not tolerate unreasonable behaviour.

Obviously this is a very extreme story told to me by a capable and reflective woman who had considered every aspect of conflict in relationships, especially with her professional background in law. You cannot fight with people who are already fighting themselves — it's possible the boy felt that to accept his stepmother meant rejecting his own deceased mother. But it also took much therapy to help this woman withstand the attacks from her stepson.

In both cases, both step-parents behaved with dignity and respect, and lost nothing by stepping down or stepping away. On the other hand, they were able to be mind minded and consider the child's mind and attitude. In both cases the step-parents did not react to the children concerned, but quietly accepted their position. In the latter case this made no difference to the stance of the young person. This is probably to do with his age, difficult personality and the sad circumstances of the loss of his parent, as older children have more to think about when it comes to parental relationships. The stepmother did the only thing she could — step out of harm's way, take good care of herself and maintain a respectful stance.

Conflict and break-ups

As this book should have helped you understand, the skill involved with being mind minded and Mind Kind is that you need to be able to consider several different states of a child's mind at once, because this is almost certainly what will be going on for them. None of our minds are one dimensional; we have many different levels of functioning that need to integrate for us to be comfortable. When older children have been part of a separation and divorce process they will have been put under some pressure and it will cause them some anxiety, however hard parents might have tried to protect their children from the process.

Broken marriage is a trauma, however much you want to separate from a person. You might have once loved that person, made an attachment to them, taken them into yourself and considered them part of your future. When these dreams get broken and families are to split up it is an enormous and very painful threat. The parental task is to make this experience as free flowing, as well understood and easy as possible for your child, while at the same time acknowledging the inevitability that there will be some pain involved in the process. It means putting your child's needs before your own but also taking your own needs very seriously. It is a very difficult time indeed for all concerned and nobody gets off without some stress or distress. You will have to be mindful of this and attend to your child's thoughts and feelings about separation in a Mind Kind way.

There is no doubt that age is a great protector and that some aspects of a break-up will mercifully fly over the heads of young children just as long as they have not been witness to violence, arguments, great distress, unkindness, abuse or too much anxiety. Observation of any of these behaviours will affect young children for the rest of their lives as it will frighten them. If they see any parent being harmed it will cause them trauma — even if they hear you arguing it could traumatize them, so close proximity to a couple fighting and in conflict is no place for children. If you have to argue, which is quite likely, at least be mind minded enough to make sure that your children are out of the way and cannot hear. Even then they will pick up on an atmosphere of hostility between you. The rule is to keep conflict out of their way as soon as possible and to separate if you cannot bring harmony into your home. Harmony is what children require if they are to grow and develop in a happy way. If you cannot provide an environment with harmony then you might need help with this key aspect of parenting. Environment is everything and attention to emotional states is fundamental to wellbeing.

Older children will be able to evaluate the state of the parental relationship quite quickly and they might feel they have to take sides or protect the more vulnerable parent. They are highly likely to feel they are in some way to blame for the break-up. They will be quick to perceive unfairness and you might like to be aware that if you hurt your partner you are effectively hurting your child.

With all the emotional and financial issues and changes in the home, you need to be careful that children are kept safe and not lost in this process. It is hardly surprising that many children get bewildered at this time, even when they have the most loving parents who are doing their best.

Half for you and half for me

Through working in the court system I have seen parents make hard choices on how to care for children once separation has happened. Some parents seem to be of the mindset that children are a commodity that should be split evenly between them on a minute-by-minute basis. Many parents may feel pleased with themselves and feel that life has regained its fairness when they have achieved an equal half of their share of the kids; so the children might spend half the week with one parent and half the week with the other. The parents are happy, but they don't stop to think what it is like to split yourself between two homes.

For the record, I think this is not always a mind-minded solution, as it may not take your child's emotional needs into consideration. Instead, the very first consideration should be: 'What solution gives least inconvenience and upheaval to this child?' The child remaining in the home that they know and feel familiar with is a priority, as is remaining in the school that they know. It is very disruptive to make your child move school due to a break-up and very unfair for them to lose their friends and familiar surroundings. Thus, if one parent is staying in the parental home with the children, they are very fortunate indeed and perhaps should consider what it might be like to be the parent who has had to leave that security. Of course, it is essential that the partner who moves out should remain present for the children and in their lives, but it does not mean that the children should be dragged out of their home for exactly half the week. Many children who have to do this eventually become resentful and depressed if they are treated as commodities. In terms of mind mindedness, I have seen some dubious solutions to the problem of 'getting a fair share' and I am going to name them so that if you are considering similar solutions you might like to reflect carefully on whether they are fair for the child.

» The child gets sent to a boarding school that is equidistant from either parent so that neither parent gets more than the other. The child's time is equally split on return home during the holidays.

» The child travels a long distance every weekend so that the other partner gets their fair share. The parents argue over who is to pay for petrol for the travelling and so some weekends are stopped anyway.

» The child gets to travel a long distance after school one evening so that an exact mid-week split can be established with not one extra hour to the other parent.

» The child gets dropped outside a public library, with video cameras, when going to the other parent so that if the parents do get into an argument it can be recorded to see who started it.

» The child walks 500 metres on their own to the other parent's car so that the parents do not have to see each other and so they do not argue.

» The child is not allowed to transfer items from one home to the other so the other parent cannot harm or destroy the items. There is one set of clothes for one home and one set for another.

» New items given in one home are not allowed to be taken to the other home by the child (e.g. pyjamas, coats and toys). So the child has one coat for three days and another coat in another home for the other days.

I think I will have made my point. All of the above solutions were made by perfectly able and intelligent parents who had lost their perspective and forgotten to put their child's emotional needs first.

All of these problems can go to mediation and get sorted out through conflict management if the parents cannot find a way between them. We quickly have to face up to the skill of managing conflict. All that is really required is a good plan for the future and a primary recognition that the emotional, mental and physical needs of your child are paramount to your own. You might miss out on a day or two and you may feel that you have to surrender a little, but your child will be happy. You have to ask yourself if you want to be right or if you want your child to be happy and feel free to love you when they see you.

Mediation and conflict management

We are establishing a pattern of thinking here that gives parents options about the way they behave with their children. I propose throughout this book that if we understand human behaviour and human development we are more likely to understand our children as they evolve through life with changing needs and patterns of behaviour.

If we truly understand human behaviour, it is not so very hard to understand why people fall into conflict. Conflict occurs when our mindset does not accord with the mindset of another, when we are unable to establish a win–win scenario in which everybody has their thoughts and feelings acknowledged and attempts are made at compromise. Successful relationships depend on this formulation and will frequently be put to the test in terms of understanding and management. Successful relationships will go through periods of adversity and conflict but will come through because a desire for harmony and understanding is achieved. This does not make you a bad person if you do not achieve this goal. Sometimes we have to walk away from situations in order to achieve peace and harmony. So to leave a situation where you cannot win and cannot get your needs met, despite your best efforts, is probably the wisest thing to do. But it is almost impossible to do this if you are in a relationship. You cannot just walk out of a relationship because a stepchild is difficult and generally children cannot walk out of the relationship with their parents (although sometimes we do see them do this). This sense of a double bind creates an anxious and traumatic state of mind for parents, step-parents, children and stepchildren alike.

To manage conflict is the apex of achievement for the human species that differentiates us from animals who simply fight their way to a conclusion if necessary. That is not what humans have evolved to do. It's easy when we get along together, but it's not easy to negotiate and create a dialogue on difference and be mindful of the rights of others. That is truly what makes us civilized. It is in a civilized society, where we face up to conflict through due process, that we are able to flourish and get on with solving some real problems. As we go through life we learn to adapt, flex and truly learn the art of managing conflict. And in doing so we know that we have grown up, developed and evolved rather a lot. We teach our children to manage conflict as they go through life, from the small moans about their friends who let them down, to dealing with mean behaviour from other children and learning how to manage our own reactions that can lead to aggression. Children who have received this tutoring from patient parents who create a Mind Kind dialogue about managing differences are very fortunate. This openness of mind makes them social children who will be liked, and it will make them resilient and stable in the face of adversity. Most of all, it is children who are mindful of the need for self-management and finding solutions who are likely to remain empathic during difficulty and not rebound into a fight or flight response. Whatever their IQ, children who have learnt these skills will be social winners. My main point in this chapter is that all of this can and must be learnt within the world of stepfamily and step-parenting and it has to be learnt quite quickly.

However, there is one trap that you must be particularly aware of ...

I hate you and so will my child

Sadly, I have been in court on many occasions with couples who are at war with each other for years. They just cannot let go of the fight and in my view may be finding it hard to let go of controlling each other or even their underlying attachment to each other. It becomes apparent that people have lost their pride and independence and believe that the primitive mechanism of fighting through the sophisticated court system will sort it out. It rarely does in family matters of this nature.

If a court has to make a decision about where a child will be at what time, this indicates that you have been unable to compromise and negotiate this and in my view this is a parental failure. Unfortunately, some couples actually resort to dragging their child into the argument, asking children to choose who they would like to be with and even compelling children into situations where they mistrust the other parent, including false allegations about that parent. The impact of this on children is similar to that of children who have to live in a war zone. They become isolated, possibly alienated from their family, and because nobody is noticing, the children simply have to find their own ways to survive. Like a war, this can go on for years.

To alienate a child from a parent due to real circumstances of danger or concern is quite a separate matter, but to alienate a child from a parent simply because you have fallen out of love with them is a matter of conscience as well as mind mindedness. By doing this you may be depriving your child of their human rights. The fact is, all children have the right to love both parents, and to deprive them of this reality is cruel and unkind, and deprives them of their right to love freely. It also demonstrates on your part a lack of ability to understand a child's mind and their needs. If you feel the need to engage in this sort of behaviour without real reason, then you may need to take support or advice on the effect it has on your children and the toll it will take on you.

◢◢◢

In conclusion

With all these conflicting issues potentially in the mix, it is small wonder that children may end up with a rucksack full of psychological anxieties about new step-parents, feeling protective towards their own parents and needing desperately to feel more secure.

It's hard to be Mind Kind to a child if they frustrate you or even hate you, but the rules remain the same. You have to find your peace of mind from somewhere. It is my view that step-parents need support with the Mind Kind journey and that the journey is as much their territory as anyone else's. They need to be careful not to fall into the trap of becoming the disgruntled other in the child's life. This rather makes all the fairytales come true. And birth parents have an important role to play in supporting step-parents and children in their journey together. It is also my view that many step-parent and child relationships fail because birth parents are not mind minded enough or do not work hard enough to put things right or take the time to try to understand the complex scenarios in which the people they love most in life have found themselves.

Ultimately, there is a lot of work to do together in the mix of family change and stepfamilies.

Self-image, self-worth and eating

I have devoted a whole chapter to this subject because I think it is one of the big issues of our time, for our society and culture, for ourselves as individuals and, crucially, for our children. This chapter is a generic view of why people overeat or undereat, and it looks at how eating is linked to our self-worth and our relationship with our bodies.

Facing up to fat

We can tackle the issue of obesity within society on many levels. We can think of overweight people as the product of a world in which we have become victims of our own socialization and efficiency. We don't have to run and catch our food or hunt for it and there is plenty of it available. The obesity epidemic is not because we choose to be fat and greedy. It is because we work hard at storing and harvesting and we have become expert at doing this. But the fact is that overeating and being overweight has become an issue, largely because we have an awareness problem around food. However, there is no doubt that just as step-parents come with a bit of mythical baggage attached to their role, overweight people also carry mythical baggage around being heavy. That baggage is often painful and unfair, and it is especially unfair to heavy children.

Perversely, in modern industrial societies we receive a strange and confusing message: we have plenty and you can eat all you want, it's just that you will become overweight and you won't be attractive, and nobody will love you. But this is inaccurate — if about half of us are predicted to be overweight by 2030 that would mean an awful lot of us not being in successful relationships. I don't see that being true. I do see a lot of really heavy people being loved for who they are and living in successful relationships.

Food is part of our relationship with others. The first thing we do with our newborn children to show them that we want them to survive and they are loved and cared for is feed them as much as they need. So from the moment we are born, food becomes a metaphor or a substitute for how much we are loved and cared for, and how safe we are in our primary relationships. As we grow, food becomes the medium through which we are able to care for ourselves. We are deeply influenced by our society, and our industrialized society takes control of our eating, much as a parent does with a child. It takes control by knowing exactly what it puts into foodstuffs that we eat but not letting you know too easily what you are eating. Thus, the seventeen teaspoons of sugar in the average soft drink or soda is not exactly written clearly on the front of the can. Since information is power, it stands to reason that there is a certain amount of power that the food industry holds over us. This is no longer just a matter of life and death, it has become another form of survival — economic survival. Food is no longer considered simply part of an ecosystem in a natural experience; it is embedded into our social and economic system and as we are all part of that system it is rooted in our thinking and behaviour.

There are multiple layers to the problem of food and self-image with children. Parents are just so busy. Mums are not standing at home any more wondering how to use last night's leftovers to create a healthy and economic family dinner. Instead, many parents and carers rush for ready-made food on their way home from demanding jobs just to be with their children, the loves of their lives who have been feeding themselves on ready-made snacks while waiting for the adults to get home. Busy parents just don't have time enough to check whether their children are getting enough exercise or calculate the calories their children have consumed and burned that day or how many teaspoons of sugar they have taken. Kids get trapped in front of computer games with no release for their bodies and they get stuck in an unhealthy cycle of behaviour. Even if they don't put on weight, they are certainly dysregulating their system with too much electronic light that will affect their sleep and make them irritable. And we can't be sure with all of this food that they are getting the nutrients that they need. So if children are not frustrated or worried because they feel they are putting on weight, they are frustrated anyway because the balance of their lives just is not right.

It could be said that our scales don't balance because our systems are not balancing, and it takes one big thrust of commitment to turn any one of these systems around and start a new style of behaviour, especially when you are only one person in a big economic process. The ethos in which we live is geared to minimum movement and effort combined with maximum indulgence and choice. It is too much for children's bodies and too much for their minds, unless we can help them to take control. Unfortunately, not only have we created a major systemic, political and economic problem around food and lifestyle, but we have also created a massive problem around image and self. While the food system feeds us up in a distorted way, the image system feeds our minds with images of perfection and unreachable levels of thinness that make even average-weight children feel they are too fat. Impossible and perfect images set us up to fail and they flood into our children's minds continuously.

I started working as a psychotherapist 25 years ago by focusing on weight and self-image issues for women, and since then the problems have remained just the same. Twenty years ago I was pointing out that fashion dolls were getting thinner. Today they are even thinner and also very sexualized too — there is now even a thin model-style doll who pole dances. So it appears to me that nobody in advertising, politics, economics or even psychology listened to the warnings that we were putting too much pressure on people to be thin. The situation now involves men as much as women, men who are required to be thin but to have muscles and six packs to show off their masculinity. So how can we recover from this and protect our children from taking in these compelling pictures?

Parents feel anxious for their children when they become overweight because they know the psychological and emotional pain to which they will be introduced, in the form of comment, criticism and self-doubt. It is not as if parents go out of their way to get their children fat and yet it is the hardest thing of all to turn around, because you know that you are going to have to stop your child from eating things they think they enjoy (certainly at first anyway). There is, in addition, the rather unfair predisposition that some children have — the weighty gene that makes some of us more prone to fat than others. Some of us are predestined to have to weight-watch. The fact is that if you have a child who is like this, or if you have this tendency, you are going to have to face up to the problem in just the same way as you would any other problem with a child. In the Mind Kind style, the journey starts with your thoughts about the matter so that you can manage a skilled life change for your family, your child and probably yourself, rather than a clumsy, hurtful declaration about the state of a child's body, which sadly I have witnessed too often.

Ultimately you will come to realize that the journey starts with thinking about food, and the source of that journey is your mind, yourself, your values and how sensitive you are to the needs of your body. This includes the need for food but also for other things: rest, exercise, fun, freedom, sleep, interests, belonging, love, security and achievement. Food is a single part of a whole package that your body and mind needs. Food is part of a journey of self-care and self-esteem, and that journey for children can only start with you as a parent and the style of your care. You could ask a simple question of yourself — 'What do I think about food?' — and notice your mental responses to that: 'I could not care less', 'I live to eat', 'Whatever', 'I'm too busy'. The relationship you have with food will start with these thoughts. Again, there is a balance to strike here. It is the balance between raising children who are neurotic foodies to children who will stuff anything down them without thinking. Neither position is particularly desirable. What we are looking for is a child's intake of nourishment, their enjoyment of that nourishment and a growing sense of responsibility and mindful respect to their relationship with their body and food.

If you are worried about your child's weight or their relationship with food it will really help for you to externalize those thoughts, perhaps with a counsellor who works with children and obesity or with your GP or a thoughtful friend. Obviously the last thing you want to do is cause issues of shame and humiliation for your child, so I suggest you think through all of your thoughts first before you decide how you are going to change your child's environment. This will help minimize any guilt they might feel about their weight and any responsibility for solving a problem over which, as a child, they cannot take ultimate control. This would leave them with anxiety and despairing thoughts. The problem is, without doubt, much more than half yours. So while a child might have to get used to some new tastes in food and a new pattern of eating, they certainly don't have to worry about what they are doing right or wrong, or most of all that it is their fault. Let's be Mind Kind clear — it is not their fault and the task is to help and support them to make constructive change.

Where to start

The first place to start when wanting to make such changes is to let your child know that you accept them exactly as they are right now. This is the most powerful place to begin if you want to change anything. Do not give the impression that you will love them more when they've lost a bit of weight. The message is: I love you now, you are mine, you are adorable, you have so many talents and skills and you are beautiful; let's face this challenge of balancing your food intake so that you can feel good about yourself every day. This is a bold place to start and suggests the problem is already half solved.

This message is so very important to the motivation to change, yet it seems paradoxical, so let's get clear about this. Making changes is so much easier in a positive psychological climate when we are feeling softer and more accepting of ourselves. It is much easier to change when we are less fearful about things such as our status, how loved we are and how safe we are. If children are overweight the last thing they need to feel is that their parent hates them and is disgusted by them because they have become too big. This means that their last vestige of psychological safety has been taken away and they feel even less deserving of feeling good than they might have done before. You will achieve nothing by stating the obvious 'You are too fat' until you have dealt with the emotions of love and security that go with this condition. Your child will know if they are fat. They don't need you to tell them. There will be any number of people who will be ignorant and unkind enough to your child so don't make yourself one of them. Statements like 'Hello gorgeous, let's see what we can do together on this' are going to be far more encouraging.

Building motivation requires a very specific frame of mind. Here I am mindful of the work of Steve Rollnick and William Miller on making changes.[1] Although now 35 years old, it is still as relevant today as ever as a framework for helping us to think about how to make change in our behaviour. In their work on increasing motivation (which was really intended to help with drug and alcohol addiction but has many applications including helping children with behaviour), Rollnick and Miller remind us of the conditions for change, which have been proposed in the work of so many psychological therapies starting with Carl Rogers, who was a psychiatrist working with children.[2] In fact, the motivational interviewing framework borrows from many schools of psychological thought, ranging from the theory of ambivalence to research on self-regulation.

Motivational interviewing is a style of engaging with people who need to make changes in their lives, especially if they are involved in addictive behaviour that is harmful to them. It particularly focuses on the way that we engage and speak with people to help and support them to change patterns of behaviour. Over the years it has proven to be a simple yet extremely effective technique.

Primarily, the problem is not food — and it is more likely to be your indifference to the information about food that is the cause of the problem. So, the act of ignoring that you have a problem with your child is the actual issue, rather than the overweight child themself. The difficulty is that there is an awful moment of discomfort when you realize you have a problem. That 'oh no' upset experience — I am not worthy and I am getting something wrong — is just awful to feel. But it is the point of change. All weight-watching adults who have had to step on the scales and realize the extent of their weight increase have been there. You know exactly that awful 'I am a fat person and my life is out of control' moment of panic.

There is no need for children to have to suffer this excessive sense of shame about themselves if they are overweight. It is shame that makes us hide the problem and pretend it is not there. It is our job to give our children hope straightaway so that they can do something about this situation, thus increasing a sense of 'I can' rather than a sense of shame. That is why motivational interviewing proposes that there are some critical conditions we need to experience in order to make changes. One of these conditions is empathy, closely followed by unconditional positive regard, with honesty and authentic communication following a close third. So to deal with the terror of the monster referred to as the scales we must apply some very 'You are worthy' messages to encourage our child to wish to take control, with your help, and make a plan for change. A great way to do this is to go through the process yourself and demonstrate it to your child in order to start the conversation. 'I felt so bad when I got on the scales as I knew I had put on weight but here goes — I'm going to enjoy eating great food and cutting back on the junk so I can feel good again.' Or perhaps, 'I really need to move more and I have a new plan for movement each day — I feel really excited about this as it will help me feel better and shift my weight.'

Most children are just dying for a chance to deal with any weight problem and for someone to give them real hope and encouragement. Even just starting the conversation could encourage the average child to say, 'I feel really bad about my weight too.' However, children are so alert to communication and they will know if you are patronizing them with false information. You had better get your authenticity act together — in reality, where are you with this problem? A lot of children I meet who have difficulties with weight feel that their parents have a problem that they cannot solve for them. This also applies to children and young people who choose to diet to extremes; often they feel that their parents are doing the same and this influences them.

Rollnick and Miller offer keys to change with this problem. They say that 'a diagnostic label in itself does not predict change', (i.e. saying to your child 'You're fat' is unlikely to do it). But the following ideas may help very well indeed:

Give advice

Talk to your child or get a counsellor on nutrition for your child to talk with if you think you are going to be hopelessly inept at the job. A single session of counselling or information about weight and food should increase your chances of making a change from 5 per cent to 65 per cent. So, information about making a change in eating patterns and exercise may be helpful. For example, talking with a child about developing a form of exercise that they enjoy is a great way to go, or explaining that sugar needs to be limited.

Deal with barriers

Help your child deal with any barriers. Human beings can be amazingly adept at the craft of creating psychological barriers so that they don't have to make changes. We love our comfort zones so much. Any good coach will know that you need to lovingly and mindfully attend to these barriers through conversation before attempting to make any change. Here is the most common barrier: 'I don't have time to make change!' You can always make time.

Choice

It is so important that children are given a sense of power over any situation with weight. This can be achieved by giving them a range of options from which they can choose with regard to exercise and food. Choice and responsibility will motivate your child more than anything and give them a sense of power over the problem rather than the problem having power over them. This will also leave them feeling that you believe in them.

I am referring to children over the age of seven (middle childhood and onwards) because we cannot expect babies, toddlers and preschoolers to have the capacity of mind to make too much choice for themselves. In their little cases it is easier to change their lifestyle in a way that is joyful to them and not punishing. With older children, once that good news has been absorbed — that they get a choice about which foods they feel they can cut out and swap with healthier options — you can sit and plan with them.

Desirability

How desirable can you make both exercise and less calorific food for your child? This is your new mission. There is no need for children to be hungry to lose weight and there is no need for an excessively draconian diet. This would be unkind and would not work. Children need to learn to be comfortably full rather than stuffed and they need to learn how this feels for at least a few weeks before they adapt. They may go to bed feeling a little lighter but not starved.

There needs to be a good balance when beefing up the desirability of a more well-balanced regimen. For instance, thinking of the most desirable fruits to eat and putting them on the list of 'can have' rather than thinking of all the things that have got to go. But really what we are looking at here is getting your child to see the favourability of change by making a good plan. You also have to convince yourself of this, because there is no doubt that the first few weeks of a regimen change are going to be hard work for you (and your partner) and you are going to have to be a more empathic parent, more supportive and very involved, until your child is an agent in control of the new plan. Increase the desirability of the new and decrease the desirability of the old ways with food.

Empathy

I hope we have established the basic principle that we are likely to achieve more through kindness than through harshness with our children. Kindness is the number one tool in the therapist's or parents' tool bag to get change. Our warmth, our respect, our supportiveness and our understanding all have to be in place. If you cannot find these states within yourself then take a break — you need to think more about this situation and to really understand the problem for your child. If you can't find any empathy then find someone (qualified and safe) who can.

Goal-setting

You need to set regular goals for your child to achieve in this new pattern of behaviour. I would be careful not to make these necessarily weight orientated, because weight will not necessarily drop immediately; it might take a month for your child's body to adjust before their weight changes and you don't want them to be disappointed. It's best to reward your child for sticking to a new exercise regimen such as walking to school and cutting back on certain foods in the early stages.

If weight loss is happening, then this is a bonus. Having said this, weekly weighing is a great motivator and children like to watch numbers and do the maths. So if your child is dropping pounds you can set weight goals, but I would suggest at a very slow rate of no more than ½ kilogram (1 lb) per week, which is the average healthy weight loss advocated by most weight loss organizations. Do not set your child up to fail and explain to them that they won't necessarily lose a lot of weight at first but that they will just feel better.

Continual disappointment at not losing weight does not have to hamper their motivation when there are so many other areas of focus where they can achieve.

Just be helpful

Help your child keep away from junk food and unrefined carbohydrate by not buying it or keeping it in the house. Try, as much as possible, to prepare food that is low in these carbohydrates and sugar but at the same time delicious and filling — this will always include healthier carbohydrates such as pulses, which are high in fibre, have a low glycaemic index (GI) and contain filling protein. This, combined with a wide variety of vegetables with smaller amounts of protein and healthy oils and fats such as in avocado, oily fish, nuts and olive oil, provides a nourishing and delicious array of food. This approach to eating constitutes a Mediterranean-style diet, which is considered to be most beneficial to the body.

If we did not know it already, evidence suggests that sugar is the real killer product with regard to weight control, and reducing intake will make a massive difference to their calorie intake. Even fruit juices are too high in sugar so try to help children to stick to drinking water. Find some way to make vegetables more delicious so that children will eat heaps of them. Let children get interested in their own food by learning to cook. Get children to make their own bread and pasta. Stick to wholemeal products rather than highly refined products or use half and half products to entice towards wholemeal. Help them with their exercise — if you can be with them when they do this, then that is great. Give them an opportunity to talk about and be excited about this change in their lives.

Avoid arguments and roll with resistance

There are a few other rules of Rollnick and Miller's motivational interviewing that can be very helpful with changing eating habits (and also as general rules for parenting older children). I always call this rule one of parenting: if you are arguing with your child, you are getting it wrong (see 'Arguing with your kids' on p. 147). Motivational interviewing style is to 'avoid arguments and defensive behaviour' because the problem will get worse. Remember: who is the adult here and who ultimately has all the power? You, of course.

If you are arguing it is because you are defensive. Your child can argue as much as they like, but do not engage with them in an argumentative way. Arguing is always a sign to lower the barrier of your discussion, not a sign to make it higher. Arguments mean that your child needs a moment to think and gather their dignity, that you are pushing them too far. The idea is to get children on board, not make them feel bad about themselves. This does not exclude a sensible narrative or discussion, which is not the same as an argument — a discussion is when two parties are engaged and hearing each other. If your conversation with your child turns into a 'telling-off' session, forget it, you have lost the game there. Just shift the focus of the conversation and come back to it later when you are feeling better and have dealt with your emotions. This includes accepting your child's emotional states on the matter and using your empathy to understand how upset they feel. I know of no child who feels happy to be overweight and we need to be able to tolerate that unhappiness.

Issues underlying misuse of food

By now I hope we have established a way of thinking: that food is about how we are, not just about a behaviour we engage in on a daily basis to stay alive. Food is a kind of emotion too. Food can say we feel bad and don't want to eat or we feel bad and don't care what we eat. Good food and good eating means being in touch with your body. It means being in touch with the physiology and biology of yourself through a medium called hunger. It is, of course, deeply satisfying to eat when you are hungry, to stop when you have had enough and get on with a life that is fulfilling. But what if your life is not fulfilling? Our response to food can just as easily be a clear indicator that something is wrong. Thus, when we are ill our bodies reject food and say to us, 'No thanks I am handling something else relating to survival at present — like my emotions or my body being sick.' The same happens if we are grieving or depressed, or going through a crisis. Food becomes secondary to the rapid progression and activity of our mind–body relationship and then resettles when we feel well or safe.

Equally, food can be used as a defence system between ourselves and what our body is telling us about life when we don't want to listen. Stuffing without thought can tell us that our lives are out of control and that we don't want to hear our emotions. This behaviour may get us through a period of adversity and when we are through it we may get back in touch with our bodies and feel better again. On the other hand, we might just carry on stuffing as it has become a habit. Either way, stuffing or starving is more often than not about a state of mind or even just a habit that does not want to listen to the body.

Children can eat or starve when they are bored, lonely, fed up, upset, anxious, frightened, confused or even traumatized by something or abused in some way. The stomach has been referred to as our 'second mind' and can be a strong indicator of how we are emotionally. These states can range from very minor events such as Mum and Dad working too hard and not having time to spend with the children, to showing us a child is unwell, to a child giving messages about a difficult situation about which they are worried. As a concerned parent you will undoubtedly feel anxious if you sense that there is something wrong with your child as indicated through their change in eating habits, but it could just be the matter of a conversation and more enquiry about their life. Either way, take note of children's eating patterns and this will tell you a lot about how your child is thinking and feeling.

The process of taking in food, digesting it, metabolizing the nourishment and then eliminating waste has been used as a metaphor for many aspects of human relationships. For example, taking in the things that people say, digesting them, making sense of the thoughts and rejecting unhelpful information is a similar psycho-biological process, so we cannot be surprised if our child's state of mind is reflected in the food that they eat or don't eat. This is really the Mind Kind perspective on food, self-worth and identity.

Eating disorders

Under this heading we are moving into a more extreme psychological territory where children (and adults) fall into rigid behaviours and patterns of eating that become life threatening, in that their body weight falls dangerously low so as to threaten life.

Anorexia nervosa

This is an eating disorder where the person has become extremely fearful of gaining weight, even when they are of normal weight or a low weight. This lack of intake will disturb the metabolism in girls and they will stop having their periods (although this stopping of periods is no longer considered to be the criteria for having anorexia and diagnosis is based on body mass index which, of course, also includes boys). Often aligned with this is a sense of distortion about body image so that the young person cannot accept their shape unless it is extremely thin (or so they think), although patients with anorexia will never allow themselves to reach a reasonable target.

This condition is more prevalent among the teenage population but can, rarely, affect children under the age of ten. The sufferer will go into a state of starvation in order to prevent any weight gain and the body, considering itself to be in a state of famine, shuts down on its requirement for food. A sense of natural hunger is then lost and young people can't eat because the body no longer accepts food or shows hunger. Most anorexics are very pleased about their loss of appetite. Teenagers often deny that they are losing weight or try to cover up their weight by wearing big clothes. This can also be combined with extreme physical activity in another effort to lose weight and shape up.

Often children who reach a dangerously low body weight (under a BMI of 16, but this varies between countries) will have to be hospitalized or sent to specialist units so that their weight increases. The psychological challenge is to help young people accept weight gain, which is very difficult for them, and help them to understand the state of mind that leads them to move to starvation. Young people suffering from this condition often have depression, social withdrawal, lack of sleep and suicidal thoughts and despair as they just cannot tolerate the thought of any fat and as their depleted bodies scream for food.

While a lot of young girls and boys have a preoccupation with their changing and developing bodies, and a lot have a desire to be thinner, they rarely fall into this state of starvation, which affects approximately 0.4 per cent of the population. Currently, for every ten girls who have anorexia there will be one boy. Personality styles will often dictate a vulnerability to this condition so that young people who are perhaps obsessive and compulsive in nature, have tendencies towards perfection, may want to control events around them and can be rigid in their thinking style, might be more prone. They may be restrained emotionally and may be introverted in nature. They may find it hard to fit in socially, feeling as if they are different and they may have suffered with this idea for many years. Sometimes attempts to be thin are a way to try to be part of what they perceive to be joining in and acceptable.

Bulimia nervosa

Bulimic behaviours include episodes of binge eating on extra-large portions of food with a sense that the sufferer has no control over what they are eating. There is still a fear of weight gain and in order to prevent this young people will then make themselves vomit or misuse laxatives, swallow salt or take diuretics or engage in periods of extreme exercise in order to remain thin. Bulimia tends to be diagnosed when episodes occur at least once a week for three months. All of this behaviour tends to be in secret as it causes a sense of shame to the sufferer.

As with anorexia and other forms of dysfunctional eating, bulimia can be triggered by negative feelings about the self, distress over life events and even boredom, depression and excessive anxiety. Young people with this condition place emphasis on body shape being a source of self-esteem and therefore they wish to maintain a perfect shape. They are often more discontent with the emotional state of their lives than their actual bodies once the issues are truly recognized. Ultimately, the act of binging does not take away the underlying distress. There are often other conditions linked to the bulimic tendency and these include depression, mood disturbance disorders and possibly tendencies to bipolar disorder, in which mood states are very extreme.

Positive self-image and self-esteem

Self-esteem is an overall evaluation that we make of ourselves. It is definitely linked to our feelings about our bodies as well as our achievements in the world. Ideally, the sense we have of ourselves is that we are good enough and sufficient. We are not looking for superlatives such as 'Hey, I'm fantastic', because these are fleeting states of mind due to something constructive having been achieved. Rather, it is the abiding sense that we have of our being in the world, that we look and feel acceptable and we are managing ourselves individually and within a social world that makes for positive self-esteem. Self-esteem is managing the difference between how I am and how I would like to be in life. Hopefully we reach a state where we have a realistic evaluation of all aspects of our self and all in all we come out feeling just fine — knowing what we are good at, knowing where our weaknesses lie and knowing what we want to learn about in life and achieve, with goals to look forward to. Self-esteem is not about feeling on top of things all the time, which is impossible. It is about the sense that you are effective at putting things back in order when needed — including your own thoughts. Self-esteem is an enduring sense of liking ourselves as opposed to self-rejection and self-hatred.

The image that we have of our self is based on the way we see ourselves and the way that we think other people see us. Thus, when I help children with their self-concept and they come out with comments like 'I am ugly, horrible and nobody likes me', I know that we are looking at a child who, for some reason, is turning negative statements towards themselves and has poor self-esteem and poor self-image. I really want to know why that is so that I can help them, but I have to help them change those self-statements into something less painful. Sometimes children will throw in negative statements because they are not used to evaluating and talking about themselves in a positive light. They are not used to the question 'How are you today?' This question is the first act of mindfulness that I like to see in healthy children who have a good sense of their inner life (for children seven years and older), a good relationship with themselves, their parents and a sense of resource and resiliency. It is a question that all parents could learn to ask their children to help them to think about themselves. And, of course, all parents reading this book will know by now to wait for an answer and accept any answer in an interested way. That is the start of a journey and a conversation about self-esteem.

The problem with self-esteem and the concept of self-esteem generally in our society is that it can be a little perverse. We can teach children to base their self-esteem on quite transient things like designer items, constant activity and whether you have a perfect body, look like a super model or have celebrity status. These transient things do not give us contentment or self-esteem; they simply fill our time and do not use our brains to capacity. It's true though that a new outfit for a child can be a step towards their self-esteem — suppose you are helping them to cut back on food and they lose a few pounds and you want to say, 'You look great — let's make sure you know it.' But what would be more important to the self-esteem of that child is that you made a cut-back plan in the first place and helped them stick to it. Your words would be quite enough to praise them. If you don't have any money, just stitch a dart in that skirt or those trousers and take them in a bit — you don't need to buy a new outfit to prove it. Really, self-esteem is an abiding feeling that comes from inside and is sustained through a perception of success or failure — not just when life is going well.

It's the things we say about ourselves in our heads that really influence our self-concept and how we feel. In cognitive behavioural therapy we call this self-talk.

▲▲▲

In conclusion

In inviting parents to be Mind Kind with their children in this chapter I am inviting a perspective on your child's relationship with their body and the world. As parents we have to be aware that there are many pitfalls in society today that can confuse our children and make them feel unhappy in their bodies. These include the idealistic images that they see in the media as well as living lives that are not compatible with the natural rhythms of the body. We need to help our children reclaim their bodies and their souls and be proud of themselves and be the best they can be, accepting themselves as a unique individual just as they are.

The Mind Kind approach suggests that you first gather together your own relationship with your body before you start imposing behaviours on your children. Following this, it suggests that you tread carefully and thoughtfully with them to find out the best plan that helps them to feel good and get on with being productive and happy, rather than stuck in the misery of body loathing. This requires effort, thought and planning but if you can get through parenthood and have taught your child to accept and respect their body, you will have served them well.

Child development: A journey, not a destination

Childhood is a continuing process rather than a one-stop event. Parents who are sensitive to their children will observe this process in many different ways. Children grow physically but they also grow psychologically, emotionally and as social animals. They are learning the very fine art of interacting with others in the best possible way, to ensure their survival and wellbeing. Parents sometimes forget that their children are trying to do this too, as it is an unconscious process not always in the front of our minds.

A Mind Kind response to childhood involves parents paying more attention to the journey of development rather than the destination that they feel their child should achieve. As children adapt and go through various stages they will, at times, struggle with change and become awkward and perhaps even unknown to their parents. A transitional or middle period when all is changing means that children are unsure of themselves and at these times they need much Mind Kind understanding and support, even when a parent may not recognize their changing child and might want them to be more reliable and static in their presentation. One such time would be the transition from middle childhood to puberty or puberty to the teenage years, when children struggle with changes to their body, mind and selves. Children can be reactive and even oppositional as they aggressively assert their sense of their new identity. Parents are bewildered and even annoyed at this disturbance and disruption, which can inconvenience the daily flow of life and their sense of control.

Many parents are equipped with little information about child development and are uncertain about what to expect and how to respond as their children grow and develop. One of the unhappiest errors (for the child) that parents can make is to think that their children are capable of more than is actually possible. A two-year-old does not really understand the importance of being polite; a five-year-old still does not have a good memory; and a sixteen-year-old is likely to want to sleep more. These are facts based in evidence, not myths about child behaviour. If these things are understood they can be more easily accepted, and then children can get on with the business of growing. Alternatively, if children are treated with scorn for these transitions and phases they will become ashamed and feel isolated as nature works through them.

One phase of development successfully completed (such as the toddler years) will carry over to the next stage (preschool), giving a child a solid base to build on, but it is always possible to repair development. If, for example, you have been through serious family adversity during one phase of a child's development, you might suddenly wake up to your child's real needs when you have a clearer mind and be able to attend to them. Choosing to pay attention and focus on your child 'now' with compassion and the right kind of support means it is perfectly possible to repair past insecurity. For example, children can move dramatically forward with their speech if parents start to pay more attention and talk frequently with their child (assuming there is not an organic problem). They can become emotionally more contented children if given attention in the 'present'.

This chapter is to help you to get with the Mind Kind mindset of your child at whatever age they are. It gives you clues about the focus of your activity as well as what you can expect. I have included commentary from real parents who reflect on their own parenting.

Infancy

This is normally considered the phase from birth to one year. Your baby is born with an instinct to ensure survival and this includes the ability to attract your attention and to mirror the behaviour of a caregiver. Babies love to make faces the focus of their attention, particularly yours if you are the main caregiver. While the growing attachment that develops between you is vital to their development in this first year of life, there are other forces at play. Babies are notably born with different temperaments. Some are sleepier and more easily comforted, some like constant stimulation and some like time and space on their own, whereas others like to remain close. Some of these temperament styles will seem to be intrinsic at birth, as if a baby is already born with a personality and style. This is developed by your care of the child and those early months are spent with a mother, father or main carer trying to find a rhythm and get the baby into their routine. Again, some fall into routine more easily than others. Some sleep easily and some don't, and some babies are hungrier than others.

Sleep

One of the big issues for parents in the first six months, especially with a first child, is settling into a pattern of sleep. At this stage you probably won't get enough sleep yourself and many parents become panicked or distressed over this. Ideally you might have someone to take turns with to give you help in the day so that you can sleep until your baby settles into a routine. Many people won't have this ideal level of support, and breastfeeding mums will be woken up to feed — unless they express into a bottle for their partner to feed baby, they are going to have to wake up to a hungry baby at night. This is where bottles have an advantage because partners can feed their baby, too.

Babies have no idea about time, nor do they have any rules about sleeping all night and waking all day. It takes them some time to get into this kind of routine and you need patience and organization while this occurs. In the meantime, it may feel like some primitive force is coming to get you while you stare into the darkness and nurse your baby night after night, wondering where your life has gone. Nobody is going to get you and your baby is not persecuting you. He or she is just readjusting to the very rigid social timeframes that we adults happen to think we need for sleep.

There are some harsh methodologies for getting babies to sleep at night, most of which involve leaving a crying baby so that you get your sleep. This is not a good idea, because babies cry for a reason and it is best to attend to those reasons. Crying indicates some need or other including a nappy change, hunger, discomfort or reassurance. If your baby is in pain or unwell you need to know about it as soon as possible, so it really is not a good idea to put them far away from you. It is best to have a new baby close to your bed. However, common advice suggests not having them in bed with you, as this may lead to accidents. Other sensible advice includes not letting your baby get too hot, using cellular blankets and not doonas/duvets, and making sure that they are not beside a heater. It is best for you to be there and you need to reassure yourself that this interruption will go on for a very short time. The more you can accept the change and feel comfortable, the more likely your infant will relax and settle.

I am aware that there are very strong arguments for having your baby in bed with you, and these relate to the joint regulation theory whereby an infant is influenced to feel better and safer by the heartbeat, warmth, contact and regulatory system of a parent at night-time — thus helping their own little system to be more settled. I understand this argument but the problem is that it is generally not thought to be safe to keep a tiny baby in bed with two fully grown adults. Also, if you as a parent are not getting enough sleep because you are concerned about rolling on to baby or have them snuffling at night-time (which babies often do) you are not going to be a very smiley parent the next day. So having your baby close by or next to your bed in a bassinet or cot of their own is very much a healthy and safe compromise and you don't have to travel far to know what is going on with them. Any mother, father or substitute parent will be quite close enough to meet those primitive needs of the baby's sensory system and if you are close by, your baby will smell you and that will keep them happy.

Other issues relate to pressure on the relationship between the baby's parents, which can come under stress due to the dramatic changes at this time. One parent may be more tired, while the other may feel alienated by the main carer and their relationship with the baby. There is a massive change in identity, particularly for someone who is providing the majority of care. This could be called maternal care whether it is a woman or a man. Maternal care is so essential because it refers to those qualities that are nurturing, focused on the infant, caring, attentive and protective. This takes acres of time and adaptation on the part of a parent, and changes your identity. It changes a lot of things and you definitely have to adapt to becoming a different person. You have to become less self-centred, and sometimes you want to change your friends. You also have to deal with the gushing hormones of loving and protecting a baby, which can be overwhelming. If you have been a person who has had a lot of control in your life, you could find this adaptation a bit of a call on your psychological resources. But the majority of parents fall in love with their babies within a few weeks without too much resistance, after crossing a few hurdles and learning from experience about what their baby needs.

See if you can aim for quiet and organized days in which you settle for a calm baby as your focus. If you can do this, then with a bit of time, everything else should fall back into place for you. Your baby will have episodes of frustration and upset as they settle, but you will get used to these if you can approach them with confidence and the understanding and view that your attention to them at this time is the most important part of the job.

A parent with a new baby reflects

Absolutely nobody could have told me what this was like. We were so full of ourselves going to classes for the birth — I thought, 'This is going to be easy.' At no time did I take into consideration the idea that pregnancy was quite difficult and frankly weird as so much was going on in my body. I thought that at birth all that would end and life would get back to normal. I thought babies were highly organized and could be fixed in a timeframe quite easily without questions — 'Marvellous,' I thought, 'I will be able to get on with life.'

I wonder if other types of mothers would have had a better time than me. I have been in a career for years where I have the last say. I felt broken down by the demands of my baby and could not believe any tiny creature could be so demanding of my time when I had run a department of thirty people on a budget. I think it took me six weeks to settle after the birth. As soon as I started to accept my baby's cries as normal and let baby take the lead, I started to feel better.

Toddlers

It is a good job that little people aged twelve months to three years are so adorable and appealing in nature. They are extremely busy about life and have very little motor control, which makes them adorable but very hard work indeed. You will need all your love and empathy for the frustrations you can feel about them and they can feel about you at this age if you are going to cope in a mind-minded way. Apart from in their teenage years, their brain will never be working quicker to develop. If babyhood was demanding then toddlerhood is a roller-coaster of excitement and development for your little buddy, who will trail you around the house and need your constant attention if you are the main carer. Not surprisingly, many parents escape to work as light relief and leave the job to a qualified childminder, the main task being to check that he or she is kindly, thoughtful, safety minded, that they are Mind Kind and love your small child as much as you do because they are the substitute for you during the day.

Along with the use of tiny legs comes the cognitive developmental stage of chattering. Chatter begins with toddlers sounding the universal consonant of mumumumuma that eventually sounds like Mama in so many languages or dadadadad which also sounds like Dada. This is an event so wonderful that you will think it is only you that has ever been called this name by their child, even though it has been happening for hundreds of thousands of years as an initial stage of cognitive development. But the specialness you attribute to your toddler is vital because it means that you work hard for their development by showing you are so proud of their achievements, and they in turn become proud of themselves. So using the potty after the age of two, eating food with fingers, drinking from a cup, walking combined with riding in the stroller, all become part of the accumulation of skills that contribute to the graduation ceremony into being a preschooler.

Within a year your child will have accumulated about one hundred words and be chattering to you. Most of all they will have developed the ability to be curious and to ask questions such as 'What?' and 'Why?' And they will ask you all the time about things. Although this can be wearing, with parental warmth and empathy you will be able to respond to your child, endlessly going the extra mile on answering those questions because you are absolutely delighted in their development. The truth is that the more you respond, the more positive you feel and the more your brain lights up with approval as you interface with your toddler, the more they are going to light up too and the more their brain will develop. Their development is a 'mind on mind' experience with your mind (or those close to your child) being the chief trigger for this development. This we know from the work of neuroscientists.[1,2]

Children of this age need your help to manage themselves emotionally and they are going to get cross about their limitations. They absolutely want to move forward into everything — climbing here and there, touching this and grabbing at that. They do not have good control over themselves in any sense and they are going to rely on you heavily to regulate their emotions and actions with them and help them regulate their behaviour. At this age children are known as egocentric, meaning that they really can only think in one way and that is that the world revolves around what is in their mind. It makes them appear like little dictators and all goes horribly wrong if parents get angry with their children for being this — this is the wrong response. If you can understand that they cannot behave any other way and that you simply have to help them through for a year or so until they understand more about the world, there will be massive payoffs for your patience and understanding. Children of this age are in fact desperate to be managed well. They cannot manage themselves — they need you very close by to tell them, in the most thoughtful and Mind Kind way possible, when to stop. It is up to you to be Mind Kind to your child and to yourself. Factor in breaks and make plans for time to yourself. Don't blame your child if you are exhausted.

These precious years are the root of co-operative and flexible behaviour if you can manage your responses to your child and use your patience.

Preschoolers

Children between the ages of three and five years are commonly known as preschoolers. Children of this age have an increased reliance on themselves and a better sense of self-management and regulation, but they are still predominantly dependent on their parents for support with much of their experience. They are probably potty trained by the age of three, which is a great step in management of the organic and physical self in connection with the growing cognitive brain. They are usually talking in sentences and want to relate their experiences through chattering. They have an increased awareness of their own self-agency or ability to do things for themselves and they love to achieve tasks. They are dressing themselves although the odd item may go on back to front. They are also starting to develop friendships with playmates and they love to play make-believe or pretend play games and enter into dressing up, playing social roles such as being a policewoman or a nurse.

With empathy for your child at this age and the Mind Kind attitudes you have shown throughout infancy and toddler years, your child should start now to manage some behaviour and their relationships with others. You will start to see empathic children responding kindly when they relate to other children, although they still will not be able to help their frustrations getting the better of them and they won't be able to control themselves all the time. At this age they do not engage in vengeful or mean acts on purpose and may be reactive or repeat what they have seen or learnt. Children of this age are developing their theory of mind (in which an individual understands that others have their own thoughts, opinions and points of view that may differ to the individual's) and they start to realize that other people will want different things to them. It is a challenging time for them to negotiate and they need a lot of support with understanding that life is not just all about what they want to do next. Parents who have been warm and responsive are much more likely to have children who are co-operative and love to play pro-social games (with the exception of children with neuro-developmental conditions such as autism, where socialization and relationships are more of a struggle and the child needs more help). If you were harsh and controlling with your toddler and preschooler you are now likely to see this reflected in their behaviour. However, it is absolutely the right time, with kindness, empathy and positive language, to help a preschooler turn this around. It is the right time, because in school aggressive tendencies are going to reduce a child's social competence and definitely hold them back. Pro-social children are going to be much more popular and have a happier time. So it is either time for assessment via your doctor if you are worried about your child in a social setting, or it might be time to look at your behaviour management and see if you want some help with that.

At this stage of development preschoolers need their parents to be nurturing towards them. They need their parents to teach them new things and they still need a lot of help with managing themselves and their emotions. It never surprises me that parents of children at this age seek help with understanding their children, but it is far more favourable that parents do this than run on and misunderstand their children.

Middle childhood

This is a wonderful stage of development when children start to experience their independence from you, wanting to join in with the peer group and forming close friendships, usually with other children of the same sex but not always.

Children of this age are highly dependent on support with day-to-day living but they like to feel they have some independence and a mind of their own. They will rely on you for rules, boundaries and routines, although they will challenge these and test them. They will still not remember things for themselves all the time and they will get fed up with the growing obligations they are expected to meet independently. Much of your job at this time is around supporting their sense of autonomy and functioning, while at the same time giving them a strong sense that they can return to you (their secure base) for as much support and sense of belonging as they can get. So while friendship is so vital and compelling at this stage, your child may wish to turn to you for reassurance when mishaps and disconnects occur in their relationships with others. In their friendships, children of this age are faced with the usual challenges of sharing and envy, along with issues about belonging and difference — these are vital lessons to learn for the future.

An emerging sense of identity

From the age of seven until the years of puberty, children of the phase of middle childhood start to develop a sense of an inner self and an outer self. They have a sense, then, of a psychological self that is made up of their thoughts, feelings and emotions and then they have a sense of an outer self or the image they present to the world. In total, what starts to emerge is their own identity and it is possible to ask of a child of this age 'What kind of child are you?' They will be able to respond, 'I am sporty', 'I help others', etc. This is their emerging sense of who they are. Younger children do not make this differentiation in their thinking, but it starts to become marked by the age of seven. So they may be able to talk about the two states of themselves (the inner and the outer) and begin to recognize that the inner self might have to be put on hold for the sake of the demands of the outside world. Thus a child might put on a 'face' or 'mask' at school about some anxiety in their life or they may save a difficult experience from school until they get home. They may save inner self material for conversations with their best friends and hopefully for parents and carers. Their inner self can start to represent itself in their artwork or in stories or dance. The stance for parents of children of this age is to be able to show that you love to hear about things that children want to share with you about themselves, but at the same time you respect their right to privacy and to keep their hidden self private, revealing aspects of this private self as and when they wish.

There seems to be a basic drive to stereotype gender behaviour. Freud referred to this period as the 'latency' period because children are notably asexual (without sexual drive) around this time. Boys have boys' groups and girls have girls' groups and there is a good deal of disapproval between groups for mixing. Freud saw this as a period prior to fertility and the emergence of the sexual self, when engagement in sexuality would be threatening and even harmful to a child. Consequently, there seems a natural and instinctive tendency to put up barriers. Children who want to cross barriers may be subject to teasing and made to feel different and children with any emerging sense of gender confusion need support at this time.

Friendships

Children start to evolve through their peer relationships at this age. They start to develop the notion of loyalty to a friendship group and, as a result, they also learn how it feels to cope when their loyalty is compromised. Children are making sophisticated negotiations all the time — you might think they are just out in the playground letting off steam, but in fact there is some serious business of relating going on all the time both in and out of the classroom and at home. Children are learning the balance of reciprocal relationships and the give and take of life. If you are horrible to your friend there will be an immediate consequence and great upset. If your friend is suddenly cruel and unkind you will be bewildered, and it will take much energy to put the matter right.

From parents this takes much patience. After a long day at work solving many complex problems, you are presented with 'Tabitha wouldn't talk to me today' or 'Charlie kicked me and took the ball', which may seem to have such little importance. But from a developmental perspective for your child, this is a matter of global significance and you need to respond to it as such with suggestions as to why this may be, discussing what could be going on with Tabitha or Charlie, how to manage this scenario and possible solutions to take to school tomorrow. Half an hour of your time on these diplomatic talks is the stuff of your child's future and how he or she relates to the world.

Cognitive development

Children of this age start to think more logically about life as their cognitive or thinking brain continues to develop. They really like to know how things work rather than just imagining how things work. They start to think of reality rather than just making up stories and so it becomes possible to teach history as a reality of life, their brains now being able to think along timelines. For example, as the middle years progress it will start to dawn on children that there is no such thing as Santa — they can cope with this reality because they know the difference between their imaginary mind and their logical mind.

Children now have more control over their memory but will still forget things and you cannot expect to rely totally on their memory or get angry with them about forgetting things. You can help them to remember things for themselves with prompting. Children can think about their own thinking and thus they may realize that they want to know more about a subject or that they think differently to another, or that their thinking has changed: 'I was thinking this and now I think that.' While they like logic, they have not yet got the brain capacity to think about abstract concepts. For example, a teenager could understand the ideas of communism or socialism but a child of this age (generally) cannot.

There are still limitations to the way a child can think about things between the ages of seven and fourteen, but on the plus side there is much more capacity in their mind to be able to rationalize and reason. They can make deals with you such as 'If you get your homework done I will give you a lift to your friend's house'. This is a move away from the egocentric tendencies of the toddler or preschooler where they think 'It's all about meeeeeeeeeee' (a tendency known as centration).

According to Piaget, middle years children start to have a sense of mastery and competence that leads them forward in more exploration, whereas children who have not got any sense of competence in any area may feel a sense of hopelessness.[3] The key is to watch for this sense of mastery and competence in children of this age so that it can be encouraged and transferred into teenage years. If a child is not coping with the basics of language, reading, writing and maths, then this is the best time to see if there is a problem with learning so you can boost these basic competencies. Your child may not be a child who learns academics easily and so it is important to see if they can achieve and flourish in other areas such as social skills and relationships, clubs, drama, art and sport so that they have a sense of achievement.

Teenagers

Those middle childhood years could look like a haven of organization as children move into adolescence for the period between twelve years to late teens. The rapid changes in appearance, capability and sense of self can often bring chaos to the teenage mind and are often a challenge to parents. It is a time for real understanding and respect for the pathway between complete autonomy and the desire to be supported like a child. It is a time when parents can be rejected or accepted from hour to hour and therefore it is not a good time for the insecure parent, who might need to seek support if they get 'rattled' by their crazy teenager.

Not only must teenagers deal with increased expectation, they are dealing with their developing sexual selves combined with their identity. Girls start to menstruate and boys learn about ejaculation. Can it ever get more powerful, more exciting, more primitive and frightening or more embarrassing than that? In addition, for boys there is facial hair and probably some teenage spots. For girls they have to cope with breasts and they may share the spots. Nature says, 'Look at me!' and a teenage mind says 'No, don't look at me, leave me alone, I am so self-conscious!' No wonder the mood swings increase and with it the arguments and lack of understanding. Even the most patient of parents will be pushed to their limits.

On the plus side, teenagers can be more sophisticated in their powers of reasoning and can understand more abstract concepts such as the environment, religion or politics. They are likely to be able to remember for themselves. They will be idealistic about the world and being around their evolving thinking can be a great joy to a Mind Kind parent who is prepared to listen.

Teenagers tend to start establishing their self-identity and part of this is thinking about their own uniqueness — in short, at this stage in life they cannot help thinking of themselves as rather special and very different from everybody else. They may crave attention but at the same time wish for it to go away. They might tend to feel rather transparent as the growing sense of self emerges and they can feel they are being judged and scrutinized rather too easily. This self-consciousness is an anxious time. 'Who am I and what are people thinking about me now?' are key questions that young people struggle with. Some will deny that this vulnerability exists and become tough; others will die a thousand deaths as they grapple with their emerging self and all the change it brings with it.

There is much pressure at this time to prepare for a work life, behave like an adult, engage in social roles and perform in relationships. Sixteen-year-olds can be married and engage in parenthood when they are barely out of childhood themselves. Preferably, children would have a period of respite from full responsibility during the teenage years. Practising responsibility with part-time jobs and money-making is great when you have the support of a family behind you. To learn to drive, have a bank account and engage in work are all rites of passage. Sex, drugs, cigarettes and alcohol all become a part of the teenage arena in which they have to make choices for themselves. All these big choices, including which university, which exams and who they want to be can be all too much for the developing mind. Not surprisingly there are frequent meltdowns followed by revivals and some young people really struggle with all the pressure and wish to withdraw.

Achieving an autonomous identity by the age of eighteen or 21 really depends on the way you have been allowed to build your sense of self during your lifetime. The psychological scaffolding and sense of safety that you have under you starts to show. So a boy who gets to eighteen only to discover he is gay may cope better if he has felt he has a supportive family who love him whoever he is and who throughout his lifetime have made positive comments about gay men and women. He may feel more confident about his realization if his parents have given him a real message that they love him for who he is rather than who they expect him to be. He would need them to show acceptance and support; rejection would be so painful. Often as young people approach university these identity issues start to emerge. But this change of social arena from home to university, work or apprenticeship can be another opportunity to repair any damage. Children and young people can seek out the support they need at these times from their peer group who will become even more important to them, and if universities offer good counselling and pastoral support these issues can be explored outside the home.

Parents cannot be surprised if at this stage of development peer groups hold more attraction and power than the family of origin, who may be considered unworthy of adolescent attention. This is normal and healthy, as the young person explores the outside world and challenges the childhood boundaries. It is true at this stage that boundaries just have to change. Young people must be given more freedom and normally they crave this. This is your chance to negotiate new boundaries, not an opportunity to let a child go completely. Often parents struggle with this compromise, either becoming too liberal and letting teenage children do as they please or becoming overly authoritarian and allowing children no freedom to explore. The best parents remain in a position where they are watchful and knowledgeable about what their young people are doing, even supportive and facilitative, without treating them like children. They simply wait for the opportunities when their teenagers show the need for support, then do everything they can to help them feel they can cope and show they continue to be loved unconditionally.

Adolescence is a time for idealism that needs to be accepted and valued. Young people are exploring their values in life and they are constructing their belief systems. Sometimes they are clumsy with this and may choose an unhelpful belief system. They may believe that smoking marijuana is a way to relieve stress and that it is all the good people in life who engage in recreational drugs. Either way, the only hopeful approach that responsible and authoritative parents have is that of realistic engagement, dialogue and discussion. We really can be helpful in helping young people to think, even in a five-minute conversation. The reality is that there are pluses and minuses about recreational drugs. It is a chance for young people to internalize the care that parents have for them without rejecting it. It is also an opportunity to influence the young person's emerging value system, which will hopefully move forward to self-care and respect for self in appropriate ways. I have seen even the most thoughtful of parents go through times of conflict and desperation as their young people push the boundaries in order to find themselves. What really matters is that you are still there and still caring when it is needed, rather than being rejecting and angry because you cannot control this newly emerging adult when you wish to.

The experience of a parent with teenagers

There was something so energetic and special about those years. It was so demanding and challenging to keep some sort of focus in the home with regard to boundaries and timeframes but I found it best to do this. They seemed insecure as teenagers if I was not on their case over something and at least they knew I was still there and that ordinary life went on while they went through the alternative state of teenager relationships and thinking. They were so full of idealism and hope and just nothing seemed to get in the way — not even the end-of-term exams. My husband turned into a taxi driver for them and all their friends and this was our secret weapon, as he was actually keeping an eye on where they were and who they were with. We are quite proud of this espionage — we had some control. It was also a great bartering system to get done what we wanted done.

Adult children

Parents can be surprised at how demanding it can be to parent their children once they have reached the age of maturity — old enough to vote, marry and have children of their own but not really equipped to cope with all the responsibilities that are about to befall them. This is really the test of the 'rapprochement period' (acceptance of people the way they are outside of the role of parent or child), when young people are flexing their adult muscles and at the same time still needing enough parental support to get them through a crisis. Young people of this age may move towards work and earning, and this speeds the process of independence rather more than if young people go to university whereby there is going to be some dependence on home (although I realize not all young people have the luxury of returning home with grubby washing and in need of refreshment).

Many young people will be expected to leave home at a much younger age and fend for themselves. Consequently, there is a broad range of young people from the age of eighteen (or slightly earlier) to about 24 who are experiencing the experiment of life and autonomy. Some may experience this as a playground while others are left to get on with it alone. Children who are left to fend for themselves early will commonly take up the challenge and make their young adult errors on their own or they will find friends who will support them emotionally. As a parent you have to decide how you want to do this in a way that gives your child the greatest chance possible of surviving and coping.

Ultimately, parenting is not really over. If your children go to university this might be the most costly time of your life and your hand might be forever on your credit card in supporting your young person. On the other hand, your child may choose work or other training. Whatever their choice, this is a time when your hand needs to be on the emotional credit card because your child's attitude towards you will change, and you will have to struggle with your own feelings of change, development and even rejection as your child explores independence and continues to use you as a secure base. Their own relationships flourish and their self-identity, which has been building since earlier childhood, emerges and is more defined. Young teenagers who did not explore their true identity too early, perhaps agreeing too readily with others' opinions of themselves, can struggle at this stage to experience a happiness with and acceptance of themselves. This struggle may then run unresolved through their adult years. A young man who accepts a role working in a call centre (a perfectly noble job but not his dream) when his dream was to be an accountant, might have this dream remain unexplored for the rest of his life with a sense of restlessness and discontent unless he finds a way to resolve this conflict. Equally, a young person may become an accountant because her parents wish her to be and then decide that she wishes to be a road sweeper as it gives more peace of mind. Either way, there is work to be done and dreams to be chased.

Children who adapt too easily may be hiding conflict and unresolved issues from their parents that can emerge later, although it may be easier to manage things this way. A child who has not been able to stand up to a parent and speak their mind, who has been oppressed in their opinions or who feels they have been treated unfairly (even if the parent does not see it that way) might want to revisit these experiences in adult years and certainly when they become a parent themselves. If parents can see that it is, although uncomfortable, better to have your young person ask you to face up to issues with them now, it will be more comforting for the young person concerned and for you in the long run. It is very hard to be reminded of things that have gone wrong for a parent and you might feel shame, upset and anxiety about this. But this is the time to resolve things, to see it from the young person's point of view, to use your empathy but to share your thoughts and feelings and to seek solutions and completion. You cannot put things right that you got wrong but you can acknowledge that it may have been difficult for the young person concerned. It is a mark of the strength of your parenting if an adult child can face you with these things. If you can get over your resistance to it, it could be a major, lifelong solution for you, your child and their children. They may accuse you unfairly or fail to see the bigger picture from your perspective, but you should at least seek to understand that perspective before you pile in there with excuses or self-saving defensiveness. You can also, with patience, explain your own perspective and help your child understand your story.

The view of a parent of an adult child

I found it really humiliating to be told I had got things wrong with my parenting and it upset me more than anything I can imagine. I had always tried so hard to do the right thing by my family and there were things that were wrong for them that caused them distress that I had not had time to realize. While I went through a period of feeling very upset and very down and such a failure, I eventually was able to realize that my adult child had such faith in me that they brought me in on the issue. They wanted it resolved and over.

◢◢◢

In conclusion

Development can be a confusing roller-coaster through life with challenges along the way. On the whole, though, roller-coasters are designed to be enjoyable and a thrill, and really this is what development is. As a parent you get sucked on board with your children at infancy and thrown off the train in adolescence, just when you had become used to parenting, all the time being told to keep your mind and be a provider, and now you're being told to take the psychology on board, too. It does seem rather a lot to ask. Information is everything on development and so many minor childhood states can be grasped by understanding the developmental stage of the child.

This chapter has aimed at giving you some real information, interlaced with anecdotes from parents and my view both as a parent and a professional and now in my life as a person who is committed to helping parents to parent. In my view still: the more we are kind, the more our children will have a mind.

Conclusions

Mind Kind has been written to help you support your children through life, offering parenting that prioritizes mental health and wellbeing. It seeks to help you understand your child's needs with regard to their stability and happiness rather than any other formula. It is written based on my experiences and observations from working in mental health services with 25 years of practice. Parents rush to these services in a panic when they see their children struggling with common psychological issues and they are often worried and frightened. It seems that mental health is still that 'unseen' illness that is not on a par with physical health. It is easier to respond to a nasty cold, a broken leg or even something more serious, but parents are still bewildered about mental health and nervous about their questions. The stigmatization of mental health issues within society has not receded and I believe this is because there is still not enough information available to parents (or children) to help them manage themselves and their issues.

The issue of mental health is in fact very straightforward and without mystery. My intention with this book has been to guide you through how to see into these issues that are clearly represented in a child's thinking, emotions and behaviour and their functioning in the world. It reminds us to take children seriously when they present these things to us rather than dismiss them. The workings of the mind (and consequently the brain) are available to us — the mind shows itself to us in how we think and feel, and how we eat, sleep, behave and relate to the world. Children's minds, in particular, are dictated to by the experience they receive from the outside world, and the relationship that they have with others in their world. This book points out to you, as a parent, that you are the creators and protectors of the child's world, both inner and outer, controlling the experience your child receives. It is designed to remind and help and re-empower you to help your child and to rediscover this lost world. It also sets out the practicalities of how to create an environment that is conducive to mental health and wellbeing.

This book was written to address real parents facing the everyday issues of caring for children today. It does not speak of any particular regime or totality that will immediately solve your problems for you. Instead, as a reaction to such proposals, it gives suggestions for thinking about caring for your child over time and in a mindful way that creates enduring wellbeing. The only real approach it adopts is to amplify and tease out some of the minute-by-minute issues that are going to challenge you as a parent or carer. It does not try to airbrush the very inconvenient truth that what children take is time and thought and that they require our ability to be sensitive to and attend to their needs.

So there are no magical strategies on offer. *Mind Kind* does not ask you to put your child here or there, spend a specified amount of quality time with them each day, count for five seconds for your will to be done or to sit them at the bottom of the stairs on a step when they are naughty. While these short-term strategies may offer you some sense of fleeting control, they do not address the challenge that what your child really needs to help them to cope with life is an intense set of the best kind of thoughtful interactions that you can come up with. Your child really wants you to do the best you can do for them and keep them in your mind in a thoughtful way. As I have said repeatedly, they do not need designer clothes or for you to earn a large salary, build the perfect home or provide outings to exciting places. Nor do they need you to be thin, rich or even well-educated. They need your thoughtfulness and kindness and they need to know the felt sense that you are authentic and believable when you represent this to them. If Mind Kind behaviours are not shown and demonstrated by you in a believable way, then your children will not believe you. You have to talk the talk and walk the walk. It's a lot to ask of busy parents who, in my view, need to be reminded of how to do this in the kindest possible terms.

The problem with children is that they are very authentic and immediate about this felt sense of others, particularly their parents. The felt sense just won't go away! This book has aimed to spell this out for you, showing the building blocks to security within the human mind, and in your own mind, so that you can then offer this same platform to your children. Children want to see it in their parents and they want it now. They like and crave organized, fair-minded thinking, represented in your attitude and emotions towards them, and they want it in a way that makes sense for them and gives them the best feeling in the world — to be understood and accepted by the most important person in the world to them, you. They want you to share the realities of life, their pain, distress and failure, as well as their success and joy, and life is certainly full of both polarities of emotion. They don't want to be controlled for your convenience; they want to join in the party of life with you and they want you to bring all you have to that party. They want all that support and thought, and they also want you to just be with them at times. They want to feel that you have happiness and wellbeing, too. All of these things are so much harder for parents to achieve than the latest quick fix or band-aid solution.

If parents knew the commitment that raising a child took in terms of hours, dedication, hard toil and worry they might never have signed up for the task. The Mind Kind response does not offer a get-out clause for any of these demands. In fact, it invites you to enter into the burden of parenting, rather than an expedient way to achieve it with the least possible irritation. It invites a commitment to face up to the real issues of life that children and parents experience, rather than an avoidance strategy. Evolution and life are tough experiences — birth, death, illness, ageing combined with growth, flourishing and development in equal positive and negative measure. And we are living in a fool's paradise if we do not take the hard facts of evolution seriously with our children. This unavoidable process propels us to crave the birth of babies into our lives so that we can repeat and build on our own experience with a sense of continuity and betterment. It is almost inevitable that we will have children, or, if not our own, it is likely we will care for other people's children with all our heart. I know many adults without children who care passionately for others and other people's children in their lives — it is the same evolutionary instinct 'to care' at work. We are all trying to survive under the same conditions with the same equipment and, in truth, we are programmed to experience happiness when we support others through caring and kindness. This is a marvellous instinct that has evolved to ensure the wellbeing and continuance of the human race. It is also an instinct that is one of the real joys in life that cannot be taken away from us, except of course through mental illness or prolonged despair. It could be that kindness is one of the forgotten treasures of the human mind and we need reminders about ways to awaken this latent gift.

What this book also tries to achieve is to help parents face up to reality, the coal face of parenting and see what is really going on in the development of their children. In doing this we find we need to meet children's real needs: emotion, thought and action or behaviour. I propose that, if we don't meet these immediate needs, our children will not be secure and satisfied and we will never reduce their anxiety, which is the source of most common mental health conditions in young people today.

Even if you have finished parenting and your children are fully grown, this will be an exercise in reflection on your parenting story and in many respects it is a reflection on my own parenting story. In reality, you will continue to reflect on your experience of raising children and so will your grown-up children. You may identify where you went right and where you went wrong and you may be able to talk to your children about this now. The mind is so flexible and responsive to *now*. We don't have to spend years full of regret about what might have been or what should have been. You don't have to stay stuck in what you would like to have been as a parent and the things you might like to have done. You can face your children now and change all of that through a new narrative and a fresh set of eyes. And if you are right in the middle of the parenting task, raising children and infants or teenagers now, the task is still the same and unfolding before your eyes. Give some thought to how you can improve the experience in both your thinking and theirs.

A parent reflects

When I look back on my parenting now, I realize that I knew absolutely nothing about child development and childcare and had no markers for what was helpful or not. I never had any explanation for why my child might cry for three hours one night and be perfectly happy the next day — I was just in a daze and often felt that I was getting something wrong.

I spent my parenting years with a sense of anxiety trying to think of what was going on. I had no help and nobody anyway seemed bothered to offer me 'information' about parenting (although plenty had criticism, which only served to cut me down). I wanted to make every step as easy as possible; I ended up with a child who felt I had taken something away from them: facing up to the difficulties of life. I am left saying sorry because life is much harder than I had led my child to believe.

To some extent it would be healthy to reflect on your parenting and come up with areas for development as well as areas of strength. The parent above forgot all the times she had been the best she could be and that maybe she forgot to think of herself once in a while and demonstrate to her child that she had limits herself and therefore she had to set limits. Maybe she felt she had to compensate for the lack of care in her own life at the time. Either way, she got through. My advice to this parent was to not be sorry for trying so hard and to talk with her adult child about this now.

◢◢◢

In conclusion

I wrote this book because I passionately believe that our children are our future and the way that we bring them up and care for them will be replicated by the next generation and many generations to come. I want a more sensitive society where we are more understanding of each other and this starts with understanding our children. I hope that reading this book has brought you closer to this place and put your children closer to your heart so that you, with gratitude and kindness, continue your parenting journey.

Acknowledgments

With thanks to Kate Norman for her patience and willingness to take on my mind, Tamsin Carter for the great pictures that help to illustrate the points made and Abigail Woodly for her help.

Also with love and thanks to my husband David Wright and daughter Sophie North for their belief in me and for their Mind Kind approach to life.

Endnotes

Introduction

1. Glasser, W. (1965), *Reality Therapy: A new approach to psychiatry*, New York: Harper and Row.

Chapter 1

1. Fonagy, P. et al. (2006), 'Attachment representations in school-age children: The development of the child attachment interview (CAI)', *Journal of Child Psychotherapy*, Routledge.

2. Bowlby, J. (1988), *A Secure Base*, London: Routledge.

3. Thomas A. and Chess S. (1977), *Temperament and Development*, New York: Brunner/Mazel.

4. Ainsworth, M.D.S., Blehar, M.C., Waters, E. and Wall, S. (1978), *Patterns of Attachment: A psychological study of the strange situation*, Hillsdale, NJ: Erlbaum.

Chapter 2

1. Berne, E. (1964), *Games People Play*, London: Penguin.

2. Sroufe, L.A. (2005), 'Attachment and development: A prospective, longitudinal study from birth to adulthood', *Attachment and Human Development*, 7(4): 349–68.

3. Fonagy, P., Gergely, G., Jurist, E. and Target, M. (2004), *Affect Regulation, Mentalization and the Development of the Self*, London: Karnac.

Chapter 3

1. Skinner, B.F. (1953), *Science and Human Behaviour*, New York: Macmillan.

2. Pavlov, I.P. (1927), *Conditional Reflexes* (G.V. Anrep, trans.), London: Oxford University Press.

3. Skinner, B.F. (1953).

Chapter 4

1. Faber, A. and Mazlish, E. (1980), *How to Talk so Kids will Listen and Listen so Kids will Talk,* New York: Avon Books.

2. Chissick, M. and Peacock, S. (2014), *Ladybird's Remarkable Relaxation*, London: Jessica Kingsley Publishers.

3. Enders, G. (2015), *Gut: The inside story of our body's most under-rated organ*, London: Scribe.

Chapter 5

1. www.drdansiegel.com.

2. North, J. (2014), *Mindful Therapeutic Care for Children: A guide to reflective practice*, London: Jessica Kingsley Publishers.

Chapter 7

1. Miller, W.R. and Rollnick, S. (1983), *Motivational Interviewing: Preparing people to change addictive behaviour*, New York: Guilford Press.

2. Rogers, C.R. (1961), *On Becoming a Person*, Boston, MA: Houghton Mifflin.

Chapter 8

1. Schore, A.N. (1994), *Affect Regulation and the Origin of the Self: The neurobiology of emotional development*, Hillsdale, NJ: Lawrence Eribaum Publishers.

2. Stern, D.N. (1998), *The Interpersonal World of the Infant: A view from psychoanalysis and developmental psychology*, London: Karnac.

3. Piaget's Theory in Mussen, P.H. (ed.), *Carmichael's Manual of Child Psychology*, New York: Wiley.

Index

arguing
  avoiding 187
  with children 147
  in front of children 163
  stopping 74
aromatherapy 106–8
aspirations
  lack of 141–2
  realistic 140–1
assertiveness training, for parents 145
attachment theory
  sleepwalking story 28–9
  substitute parent 155–6
attention, behaviour management 78
'attunement rule' 81
autism
  difficulty reading signals 36
  parenting needs 11
  psychiatric labels 133
avoidant behaviour
  explained 39
  from rigid parenting 134

B

babies
  are blameless 80–1
  bed-sharing 202
  brain development 49
  infancy phase 199–204
  need for attention 79
  relational brain function 48
  telling off 73–4
  urge to have 228–9
barriers, psychological 183
bed time 84
bed-sharing, with babies 202

behaviour
  assessments of 119
  avoidant pattern 39
  as communication 16
  in rigid parenting 135
  that raises risk 124–5
behaviour management
  calming down 77–8
  in class 119
  constant reinforcement 78
  emotional connection 75–6
  middle childhood years 87
  'selective ignoring' 78–9
  techniques for 71–2
  teen years 88–91
  telling children off 72–4
Berne, Eric 50
blame, misattribution of 139–40
blended families 154–6
boundaries
  changing approach to 217
  lack of 137–9, 144
  pushing 218
  testing 87
brain
  development in babies 49
  limbic system 107
  relational 48–9
bread baking 112
Brontë, Emily 156
bulimia nervosa 192
bullying, children responding to 74

C

career choice 220
challenges, dealing with 114

E

F

G

S